Contents

Tables

Mandatory Spending

Mandatory Spending (Continued)

Discretionary Spending

Discretionary Spending (Continued)

Revenues

Revenues (Continued)

Health

CHAPTER

1

Introduction

The Congress faces an array of policy choices as it confronts the prospect of large annual budget deficits and further increases in the already-large government debt that are projected to occur in coming decades under current law. To help inform lawmakers about the budgetary implications of changing federal policies, the Congressional Budget Office (CBO) periodically issues volumes of policy options and their effects on the federal budget, of which this is the most recent. The agency also issues separate reports that present policy options in particular areas.

This document provides estimates of the budgetary savings from 79 options that would decrease federal spending or increase federal revenues over the next decade. The estimates are updates of many of those presented in *Options for Reducing the Deficit: 2014 to 2023* (November 2013). The options cover a broad range of areas in the federal budget, including defense, energy, Social Security, health care programs, other benefit programs, and provisions of the tax code (see Table 1-1). The budgetary effects identified for most of the options span the 10 years from 2015 to 2024 (the period covered by CBO's baseline budget projections in 2014), although many of the options would have longer-term effects as well. This document presents options in the following categories:

■ Mandatory spending other than that for health-related programs,

■ Discretionary spending other than that for health-related programs,

■ Revenues other than those related to health, and

■ Health-related programs and revenue provisions.

For each option, this document includes a brief description of the policy involved. For additional information, including discussion of advantages and disadvantages, see the version of that option in the November 2013 volume.

This document also includes an appendix that lists options that CBO has analyzed previously but for which no budgetary estimates are presented. Those options are drawn from two sources. Some were analyzed in the November 2013 volume but would take considerable time to reanalyze; in order to make this document available prior to the beginning of the 114th Congress in January 2015, those estimates were not updated. Others, taken from various reports issued by CBO, were listed in Appendix A of last year's report.

Certain options from those two sources are omitted from this document's appendix for one of two reasons. Some have been superseded by subsequent legislation or administrative action. For others, CBO's previous estimates of budgetary savings are probably no longer useful because of changes that have been made by legislation or administrative action, economic developments, or changes in other aspects of CBO's analysis.

The options included in this document originally came from a variety of sources. Some are based on proposed legislation or on the budget proposals of various Administrations; others come from Congressional offices or from entities in the federal government or the private sector. As a collection, the options are intended to reflect a range of possibilities, not a ranking of priorities or an exhaustive list. Inclusion or exclusion of any particular option does not imply approval or disapproval by CBO, and the report makes no recommendations.

Table 1-1.

Summary Table of Options

Option	Title	Savings, 2015–2024[a] (Billions of Dollars)
	Mandatory Spending Options (Other than those for health-related programs)	
1	Change the Terms and Conditions for Federal Oil and Gas Leasing	5
2	Limit Enrollment in the Department of Agriculture Conservation Stewardship Program	6
3	Reduce Subsidies in the Crop Insurance Program	20
4	Reduce Subsidies to Fannie Mae and Freddie Mac	8
5	Reduce or Eliminate Subsidized Loans for Undergraduate Students	12 to 39
6	Eliminate the Add-On to Pell Grants That Is Funded With Mandatory Spending	76
7	Eliminate Concurrent Receipt of Retirement Pay and Disability Compensation for Disabled Veterans	112
8	Reduce the Amounts of Federal Pensions	6
9	Tighten Eligibility and Determinations of Income for the Supplemental Nutrition Assistance Program	10 to 40
10	Eliminate Subsidies for Certain Meals in the National School Lunch and School Breakfast Programs	10
11	Convert Multiple Assistance Programs for Lower-Income People Into Smaller Block Grants to States	397 [b]
12	Eliminate Supplemental Security Income Benefits for Children	103 [b]
13	Link Initial Social Security Benefits to Average Prices Instead of Average Earnings	53 to 87
14	Raise the Full Retirement Age for Social Security	35
15	Lengthen by Three Years the Computation Period for Social Security Benefits	45
16	Reduce Social Security Benefits for New Beneficiaries by 15 Percent	204
17	Eliminate Eligibility for Starting Social Security Disability Benefits at Age 62 or Later	11
18	Require Social Security Disability Insurance Applicants to Have Worked More in Recent Years	32
19	Narrow Eligibility for Veterans' Disability Compensation by Excluding Certain Disabilities Unrelated to Military Duties	20
20	Restrict VA's Individual Unemployability Benefits to Disabled Veterans Who Are Younger Than the Full Retirement Age for Social Security	16
21	Use an Alternative Measure of Inflation to Index Social Security and Other Mandatory Programs	182
	Discretionary Spending Options (Other than those for health-related programs)	
22	Cap Increases in Basic Pay for Military Service Members	24
23	Replace Some Military Personnel With Civilian Employees	20
24	Replace the Joint Strike Fighter Program With F-16s and F/A-18s	31
25	Stop Building Ford Class Aircraft Carriers	12
26	Reduce the Number of Ballistic Missile Submarines	15
27	Defer Development of a New Long-Range Bomber	26
28	Reduce Funding for International Affairs Programs	109
29	Eliminate Human Space Exploration Programs	77
30	Reduce Department of Energy Funding for Energy Technology Development	10
31	Eliminate Certain Forest Service Programs	5
32	Eliminate the International Trade Administration's Trade Promotion Activities	3
33	Limit Highway Funding to Expected Highway Revenues	82
34	Eliminate Grants to Large and Medium-Sized Airports	8
35	Eliminate Subsidies for Amtrak	14
36	Eliminate Capital Investment Grants for Transit Systems	15
37	Restrict Pell Grants to the Neediest Students	1 to 65 [b]
38	Eliminate Federal Funding for National Community Service and Senior Community Service Employment Programs	12
39	Reduce Federal Funding for the Arts and Humanities	6
40	Increase Payments by Tenants in Federally Assisted Housing	19
41	Reduce the Annual Across-the-Board Adjustment for Federal Civilian Employees' Pay	54
42	Reduce the Size of the Federal Workforce Through Attrition	49
43	Impose Fees to Cover the Cost of Government Regulations and Charge for Services Provided to the Private Sector	21
44	Repeal the Davis-Bacon Act	12
45	Eliminate or Reduce Funding for Certain Grants to State and Local Governments	54

Continued

Table 1-1.   Continued

Summary Table of Options

Option	Title	Savings, 2015–2024[a] (Billions of Dollars)
Revenue Options (Other than those related to health)		
46	Increase Individual Income Tax Rates	91 to 689
47	Implement a New Minimum Tax on Adjusted Gross Income	66
48	Raise the Tax Rates on Long-Term Capital Gains and Dividends by 2 Percentage Points	53
49	Use an Alternative Measure of Inflation to Index Some Parameters of the Tax Code	150
50	Convert the Mortgage Interest Deduction to a 15 Percent Tax Credit	113
51	Eliminate the Deduction for State and Local Taxes	1,088
52	Curtail the Deduction for Charitable Giving	213
53	Limit the Value of Itemized Deductions	64 to 139
54	Include All Income That U.S. Citizens Earn Abroad in Taxable Income	96
55	Tax Social Security and Railroad Retirement Benefits in the Same Way That Distributions From Defined Benefit Pensions Are Taxed	412
56	Further Limit Annual Contributions to Retirement Plans	83
57	Eliminate the Tax Exemption for New Qualified Private Activity Bonds	30
58	Eliminate Certain Tax Preferences for Education Expenses	150
59	Lower the Investment Income Limit for the Earned Income Tax Credit and Extend That Limit to the Refundable Portion of the Child Tax Credit	6
60	Increase the Maximum Taxable Earnings for the Social Security Payroll Tax	672
61	Increase the Payroll Tax Rate for Medicare Hospital Insurance by 1 Percentage Point	800
62	Increase Taxes That Finance the Federal Share of the Unemployment Insurance System	10 to 14
63	Increase Corporate Income Tax Rates by 1 Percentage Point	102
64	Repeal the "LIFO" and "Lower of Cost or Market" Inventory Accounting Methods	115
65	Repeal Certain Tax Preferences for Extractive Industries	15 to 21
66	Extend the Period for Depreciating the Cost of Certain Investments	241
67	Repeal the Deduction for Domestic Production Activities	190
68	Repeal the Low-Income Housing Tax Credit	39
69	Modify the Rules for the Sourcing of Income From Exports	4
70	Increase Excise Taxes on Motor Fuels by 35 Cents and Index for Inflation	469
71	Increase All Taxes on Alcoholic Beverages to $16 per Proof Gallon	66
Health Options		
72	Limit Medical Malpractice Torts	68 [b]
73	Introduce Minimum Out-of-Pocket Requirements Under TRICARE for Life	28
74	Change the Cost-Sharing Rules for Medicare and Restrict Medigap Insurance	53 to 111
75	Increase Premiums for Parts B and D of Medicare	25 to 314
76	Require Manufacturers to Pay a Minimum Rebate on Drugs Covered Under Part D of Medicare for Low-Income Beneficiaries	103
77	Modify TRICARE Enrollment Fees and Cost Sharing for Working-Age Military Retirees	19 to 73 [b]
78	Reduce or Constrain Funding for the National Institutes of Health	12 to 35
79	Increase the Excise Tax on Cigarettes by 50 Cents per Pack	35

Sources: Congressional Budget Office; staff of the Joint Committee on Taxation.

a.   For options primarily affecting mandatory spending or revenues, savings sometimes would derive from changes in both. When that is the case, the savings shown include effects on both mandatory spending and revenues. For options primarily affecting discretionary spending, the savings shown are the decrease in discretionary outlays. That same approach applies for the savings shown for health options; most are mandatory spending options or revenue options, although 77 and 78 are discretionary spending options.

For most discretionary spending options, the decrease in outlays is presented relative to CBO's baseline projections for individual components of discretionary spending, which incorporate the assumption that current appropriations continue in later years with adjustments for projected inflation. In total, the funding projected in the inflation-adjusted amounts is greater than the caps on discretionary funding. Some of the discretionary options related to defense (24, 25, 26, and 27) are measured relative to the Department of Defense's (DoD's) estimates of the costs for its plans rather than CBO's baseline projections. The costs of DoD's plans are greater than the caps on defense funding. To reduce deficits through changes in discretionary spending, lawmakers would need to reduce the statutory funding caps below the levels already established under current law or enact appropriations below those caps; the options shown could be used to accomplish either of those objectives.

b.   Savings do not encompass all budgetary effects.

Mandatory Spending

Option 1

Change the Terms and Conditions for Federal Oil and Gas Leasing

(Billions of dollars)	2015	2016	2017	2018	2019	2020	2021	2022	2023	2024	2015-2019	2015-2024
Change in Outlays	0	*	-0.4	-1.0	-0.7	-0.3	-0.8	-0.9	-0.4	-0.6	-2.1	-5.2

Notes: This option would take effect in October 2015. Estimates are relative to CBO's August 2014 baseline projections.

  * = between -$50 million and zero.

The federal government offers private businesses the opportunity to bid on leases for the development of most of the onshore and offshore oil and natural gas resources on federal lands. This option would change several aspects of those leasing programs. It would increase the acreage available for leasing by repealing the statutory prohibition on leasing in the Arctic National Wildlife Refuge and by directing the Department of the Interior to auction leases for areas on the Outer Continental Shelf that are unavailable for leasing under current administrative policies. The option also would impose a fee on all new leases of tracts from which oil or gas is not being produced. Finally, the option would eliminate payments of interest on overpayments of royalties by lessees. (Royalties are assessed on the value of oil and gas produced from leased areas.)

Option 2

Limit Enrollment in the Department of Agriculture Conservation Stewardship Program

(Billions of dollars)	2015	2016	2017	2018	2019	2020	2021	2022	2023	2024	2015-2019	2015-2024
Change in Outlays	0	*	-0.2	-0.4	-0.5	-0.7	-0.9	-1.1	-1.2	-1.4	-1.1	-6.4

Notes: This option would take effect in October 2015. Estimates are relative to CBO's August 2014 baseline projections.

  * = between -$50 million and zero.

Under the Conservation Stewardship Program, landowners enter into multiyear, renewable contracts with the Department of Agriculture to undertake various conservation measures in exchange for annual payments and technical help. This option would prohibit new enrollment in the program beginning in fiscal year 2016.

Option 3

Reduce Subsidies in the Crop Insurance Program

(Billions of dollars)	2015	2016	2017	2018	2019	2020	2021	2022	2023	2024	2015-2019	2015-2024
Change in Outlays												
Reduce premium subsidies	0	-0.1	-1.5	-1.8	-1.8	-1.9	-1.9	-2.0	-2.0	-2.0	-5.3	-15.1
Limit administrative expenses and the rate of return	0	-0.1	-0.5	-0.6	-0.6	-0.6	-0.6	-0.6	-0.6	-0.6	-1.7	-4.5
Both of the above policies	0	-0.2	-2.0	-2.3	-2.4	-2.5	-2.5	-2.6	-2.6	-2.6	-6.9	-19.7

Note: This option would take effect in June 2015. Estimates are relative to CBO's August 2014 baseline projections.

The Federal Crop Insurance Program protects farmers from losses caused by drought, floods, pest infestation, other natural disasters, and low market prices. Premium rates for federal crop insurance are set by the Department of Agriculture so that the premiums equal the expected payments to farmers for crop losses. Of total premiums, the federal government pays about 60 percent, on average, and farmers pay about 40 percent. Insurance policies purchased through the program are sold and serviced by private insurance companies, which are reimbursed by the federal government for their administrative costs. The federal government reinsures those private insurance companies by agreeing to cover some of the losses when total payouts exceed total premiums.

This option would reduce the federal government's subsidy to 40 percent of the crop insurance premiums, on average. In addition, it would limit the federal reimbursement to crop insurance companies for administrative expenses to 9.25 percent of estimated premiums (or to an average of $915 million each year for fiscal years 2016 through 2024) and limit the rate of return on investment for those companies to 12 percent each year.

Option 4

Reduce Subsidies to Fannie Mae and Freddie Mac

(Billions of dollars)	2015	2016	2017	2018	2019	2020	2021	2022	2023	2024	2015-2019	2015-2024
Change in Outlays												
Increase guarantee fees	0	-1.5	-1.4	-0.9	-0.4	-0.5	-0.2	-1.2	-1.2	-1.2	-4.2	-8.4
Decrease loan limits	0	0.1	0.1	0.1	0.1	*	-0.1	-0.8	-1.0	-1.1	0.4	-2.6
Both of the above policies[a]	0	-1.3	-1.2	-0.7	-0.4	-0.5	-0.2	-1.3	-1.3	-1.3	-3.6	-8.3

Notes: This option would take effect in October 2015. Estimates are relative to CBO's April 2014 baseline projections.

      * = between -$50 million and zero.

a. If both policies were enacted together, the total effects would be less than the sum of the effects for each policy because of interactions between the approaches.

This option includes two approaches for reducing the federal subsidies provided to Fannie Mae and Freddie Mac, two government-sponsored enterprises that were established to help ensure a stable supply of financing for residential mortgages. In the first approach, the average guarantee fee that Fannie Mae and Freddie Mac assesses on loans they include in their mortgage-backed securities (MBSs) would increase by 10 basis points (100 basis points are equivalent to 1 percentage point) beginning in October 2015. In addition, to keep guarantee fees constant after fiscal year 2021 (when an increase of 10 basis points that was put in place in 2011 is scheduled to expire), the average guarantee fee would be increased, relative to the amount under current law, by 20 basis points after 2021.

In the second approach, the maximum size of a mortgage that Fannie Mae and Freddie Mac could include in their MBSs would be reduced to $150,000 nationally, beginning with a drop to $500,000 in October 2015 and followed by a series of reductions averaging less than $50,000 a year. (Guarantee fees would remain as they are under current law.)

Option 5

Reduce or Eliminate Subsidized Loans for Undergraduate Students

(Billions of dollars)	2015	2016	2017	2018	2019	2020	2021	2022	2023	2024	2015- 2019	2015- 2024
Change in Outlays												
Restrict access to subsidized loans to students eligible for Pell grants	-0.4	-0.9	-1.2	-1.3	-1.3	-1.4	-1.4	-1.5	-1.5	-1.6	-5.1	-12.5
Eliminate subsidized loans altogether	-1.2	-2.9	-3.7	-3.9	-4.1	-4.3	-4.4	-4.5	-4.7	-4.8	-15.9	-38.6

Note: This option would take effect in July 2015. Estimates are relative to CBO's August 2014 baseline projections.

This option includes two possible changes to subsidized student loans, which, by the Congressional Budget Office's estimates, will constitute about half of the dollar volume of federal direct loans to undergraduate students for the 2014–2015 academic year. ("Subsidized loans" do not accrue interest while students are enrolled in school and during certain other periods when borrowers may defer making payments.) In the first alternative, access to subsidized loans and the associated interest subsidies would be restricted to students eligible for Pell grants. In the second alternative, subsidized loans would be eliminated altogether.

Option 6

Eliminate the Add-On to Pell Grants That Is Funded With Mandatory Spending

(Billions of dollars)	2015	2016	2017	2018	2019	2020	2021	2022	2023	2024	2015- 2019	2015- 2024
Change in Outlays	-1.7	-6.5	-7.4	-8.1	-8.2	-8.4	-8.6	-8.7	-8.9	-9.1	-32.1	-75.8

Note: This option would take effect in July 2015. Estimates are relative to CBO's August 2014 baseline projections.

The Federal Pell Grant Program is the single largest source of federal grants to low-income students for postsecondary undergraduate education. Pell grants are funded through a combination of discretionary spending (which must be appropriated by the Congress every year) and mandatory spending (which is authorized in law permanently). This option would eliminate the add-on to Pell grants, which is the portion of the Pell grant funded by mandatory spending.

Option 7

Eliminate Concurrent Receipt of Retirement Pay and Disability Compensation for Disabled Veterans

(Billions of dollars)	2015	2016	2017	2018	2019	2020	2021	2022	2023	2024	2015-2019	2015-2024
Change in Outlays	0	-10	-10	-10	-12	-13	-13	-15	-15	-14	-42	-112

Note: This option would take effect in October 2015. Estimates are relative to CBO's August 2014 baseline projections.

Two groups of retired military personnel are allowed to receive their full retirement pay from the Department of Defense without having such pay reduced dollar for dollar by the receipt of any disability compensation from the Department of Veterans Affairs (VA)—a benefit often called concurrent receipt. The first group consists of those whose disabilities arise from combat; they are eligible for combat-related special compensation. The second group consists of those who have a longevity-based retirement and have received a VA disability rating of at least 50 percent; they are eligible for what is termed concurrent retirement and disability pay. Under this option, those forms of concurrent receipt would be eliminated.

Option 8

Reduce the Amounts of Federal Pensions

(Billions of dollars)	2015	2016	2017	2018	2019	2020	2021	2022	2023	2024	2015-2019	2015-2024
Change in Outlays												
Military retirement	0	*	-0.1	-0.1	-0.2	-0.2	-0.3	-0.5	-0.5	-0.6	-0.3	-2.5
CSRS and FERS	0	*	-0.1	-0.1	-0.2	-0.3	-0.4	-0.5	-0.6	-0.8	-0.4	-3.1
Total	0	*	-0.1	-0.2	-0.4	-0.6	-0.7	-1.0	-1.2	-1.3	-0.8	-5.6

Notes: This option would take effect in January 2016. Estimates are relative to CBO's August 2014 baseline projections.

    * = between -$50 million and zero; CSRS = Civil Service Retirement System; FERS = Federal Employees Retirement System.

In fiscal year 2013, the federal government paid pension benefits of about $75 billion to civilian retirees and their survivors and roughly $55 billion to military retirees and their survivors. For civilian retirees, the size of an individual's annuity is based on the average of his or her earnings over the three consecutive years with the highest earnings. Similarly, the size of a military retiree's annuity is based on the average of his or her basic pay (not including special types of pay and allowances) over the 36 months of his or her career with the highest pay. This option would use a five-year average for civilian retirees and a 60-month average for military retirees—instead of the three-year and 36-month averages used under current law—to compute benefits for federal workers who retire beginning in January 2016.

Option 9

Tighten Eligibility and Determinations of Income for the Supplemental Nutrition Assistance Program

(Billions of dollars)	2015	2016	2017	2018	2019	2020	2021	2022	2023	2024	2015-2019	2015-2024
Change in Outlays												
Apply income and asset limits to categorically eligible households	0	-0.5	-1.2	-1.2	-1.2	-1.2	-1.2	-1.2	-1.2	-1.2	-4.2	-10.0
Apply income and asset limits to all households and further lower income eligibility limit to 100 percent of the federal poverty guidelines	0	-2.4	-4.9	-4.8	-4.7	-4.7	-4.6	-4.6	-4.6	-4.6	-16.7	-39.7

Note: This option would take effect in October 2015. Estimates are relative to CBO's August 2014 baseline projections.

The Supplemental Nutrition Assistance Program (SNAP) provides benefits to low-income households to help them purchase food. Eligibility is generally based on participation in other government assistance programs or on the income and assets of a household. Most households that receive SNAP benefits—about 90 percent in fiscal year 2011—are considered to be "categorically eligible"; that is, they automatically qualify for benefits on the basis of their participation in other federal or state programs.

Among categorically eligible households, the majority—almost three-quarters in 2011—qualify for benefits under what is termed broad-based categorical eligibility. Namely, all household members receive or are authorized to receive noncash benefits from the Temporary Assistance for Needy Families (TANF) program (such as child care, transportation assistance, or even a token benefit such as a pamphlet describing TANF).

This option has two approaches for reducing SNAP spending. The first approach would apply the standard income and asset requirements to people who would otherwise be entitled to benefits through broad-based categorical eligibility. The second approach would incorporate the first approach and also lower the income limit for all households from 130 percent of the federal poverty guidelines to 100 percent.

Option 10

Eliminate Subsidies for Certain Meals in the National School Lunch and School Breakfast Programs

(Billions of dollars)	2015	2016	2017	2018	2019	2020	2021	2022	2023	2024	2015-2019	2015-2024
Change in Outlays	-0.1	-0.7	-0.9	-1.1	-1.1	-1.2	-1.2	-1.2	-1.3	-1.4	-3.9	-10.2

Note: This option would take effect in July 2015. Estimates are relative to CBO's August 2014 baseline projections.

The National School Lunch Program and the School Breakfast Program provide funds that enable public schools, nonprofit private schools, and residential child care institutions to offer subsidized meals and snacks to students. In the 2014–2015 school year, federal subsidies are $0.59 for each lunch and $0.28 for each breakfast for many students in households with income above 185 percent of the federal poverty guidelines (commonly known as the federal poverty level, or FPL). The programs provide larger subsidies for meals served to students from households with income at or below 185 percent of the FPL. This option would eliminate the subsidies for meals served to students from households with income greater than 185 percent of the FPL.

Option 11

Convert Multiple Assistance Programs for Lower-Income People Into Smaller Block Grants to States

(Billions of dollars)	2015	2016	2017	2018	2019	2020	2021	2022	2023	2024	2015-2019	2015-2024
Change in Mandatory Outlays												
SNAP	0	-37	-35	-32	-31	-29	-28	-26	-25	-24	-134	-266
SSI	0	-9	-5	*	-5	-6	-6	-12	-7	-2	-19	-51
Child nutrition	0	-6	-7	-7	-8	-9	-9	-10	-11	-12	-28	-79
Total	0	-52	-46	-40	-44	-43	-43	-48	-43	-38	-182	-397
Change in Discretionary Outlays for SSI	0	-5	-5	-5	-5	-5	-5	-5	-6	-6	-19	-46

Notes: This option would take effect in October 2015. Estimates are relative to CBO's August 2014 projections.

SNAP = Supplemental Nutrition Assistance Program; SSI = Supplemental Security Income; * = between -$500 million and zero.

This option would convert the Supplemental Nutrition Assistance Program, the Supplemental Security Income program, and the child nutrition programs into separate, smaller block grants to the states beginning in fiscal year 2016. Each of the three block grants would provide a set amount of funding to states each year, and states would be allowed to make significant changes to the structure of the programs. The annual funding provided would equal federal outlays for each program in fiscal year 2007 increased to account for inflation (specifically, using the consumer price index for all urban consumers) since then.

Option 12

Eliminate Supplemental Security Income Benefits for Children

(Billions of dollars)	2015	2016	2017	2018	2019	2020	2021	2022	2023	2024	2015-2019	2015-2024
Change in Mandatory Outlays	0	-11	-11	-10	-11	-11	-12	-13	-12	-12	-43	-103
Change in Discretionary Outlays	0	-1	-1	-1	-1	-1	-1	-1	-1	-1	-4	-9

Note: This option would take effect in October 2015. Estimates are relative to CBO's August 2014 baseline projections.

The Supplemental Security Income (SSI) program provides cash assistance to people who are disabled, aged, or both and who have low income and few assets. Children, who make up about 15 percent of SSI recipients, can qualify for benefits if they have "marked and severe functional limitations." This option would eliminate SSI benefits for children.

Option 13

Link Initial Social Security Benefits to Average Prices Instead of Average Earnings

(Billions of dollars)	2015	2016	2017	2018	2019	2020	2021	2022	2023	2024	2015-2019	2015-2024
Change in Outlays												
Implement pure price indexing	0	*	-0.2	-0.9	-2.6	-5.4	-9.6	-15.1	-22.1	-30.6	-3.7	-86.6
Implement progressive price indexing	0	*	-0.1	-0.6	-1.6	-3.3	-5.8	-9.2	-13.5	-18.7	-2.3	-52.9

Notes: This option would take effect in January 2016. Estimates are relative to CBO's August 2014 baseline projections.

   * = between -$50 million and zero.

The Social Security Administration uses a statutory formula to compute a worker's initial benefits, and that benefit formula changes each year to account for economy-wide growth of wages through a process known as wage indexing. Average initial benefits for Social Security recipients therefore tend to grow at the same rate as do average wages.

One approach to constrain the growth of Social Security benefits would be to change the computation of initial benefits so that the real (inflation-adjusted) value of average initial benefits did not rise over time. That approach, often called "pure" price indexing, would link the growth of initial benefits to the growth of prices (as measured by changes in the consumer price index for all urban consumers) rather than to the growth of average wages, beginning with participants who became eligible for benefits in calendar year 2016.

Another approach, called "progressive" price indexing, would retain the current benefit formula for workers who had lower earnings and would reduce the growth of initial benefits for workers who had higher earnings. Under that approach, initial benefits for the 30 percent of workers with the lowest lifetime earnings would increase with average wages, as they are currently slated to do, whereas initial benefits for other workers would increase more slowly, at a rate that depended on their position in the distribution of earnings. For example, for workers whose earnings put them at the 31st percentile of the distribution, benefits would rise only slightly more slowly than average wages, whereas for the highest earners, benefits would rise with prices—as they would under pure price indexing.

Option 14

Raise the Full Retirement Age for Social Security

(Billions of dollars)	2015	2016	2017	2018	2019	2020	2021	2022	2023	2024	2015-2019	2015-2024
Change in Outlays	0	-0.2	-0.6	-1.1	-1.8	-4.2	-5.3	-6.0	-7.0	-8.7	-3.7	-34.8

Note: This option would take effect in January 2016. Estimates are relative to CBO's August 2014 baseline projections.

The age at which workers become eligible for full retirement benefits from Social Security—the full retirement age, also called the normal retirement age—depends on their year of birth. For workers born before 1938, the full retirement age was 65. (All years mentioned in this option are calendar years.) It increased in two-month increments until it reached 66 for workers born in 1943. For workers born between 1944 and 1954, the full retirement age holds at 66, but it then increases again in two-month increments until reaching 67 for workers born in 1960 or later.

Under this option, the full retirement age would increase to 67 more quickly and would then increase further. Specifically, the full retirement age would increase in two-month increments for six years, rising to 66 years and 2 months for workers born in 1954 (who turn 62 in 2016) and reaching 67 for workers born in 1959 (who turn 62 in 2021). Thereafter, it would continue to increase by two months per year until reaching 70 for workers born in 1977 or later (who turn 62 in 2039 or later). The benefits for workers who qualify for disability insurance would not be reduced under this option.

Option 15

Lengthen by Three Years the Computation Period for Social Security Benefits

(Billions of dollars)	2015	2016	2017	2018	2019	2020	2021	2022	2023	2024	2015-2019	2015-2024
Change in Outlays	0	-0.1	-0.4	-1.2	-2.3	-3.8	-5.7	-7.9	-10.4	-13.1	-4.0	-44.9

Note: This option would take effect in January 2016. Estimates are relative to CBO's August 2014 baseline projections.

As required by law, the Social Security Administration calculates retirement benefits on the basis of a worker's wage history using the worker's average indexed monthly earnings, or AIME. The current formula computes the AIME on the basis of a worker's earnings that are subject to Social Security taxes during his or her highest 35 years of earnings.

This option would lengthen the AIME computation period to 36 years for people who turn 62 in 2016, to 37 years for people who turn 62 in 2017, and to 38 years for people who turn 62 in 2018 and beyond. (All years mentioned in this option are calendar years.) The option would not change the number of years used to compute AIME amounts for disabled workers; only retirement benefits would be affected.

Option 16

Reduce Social Security Benefits for New Beneficiaries by 15 Percent

(Billions of dollars)	2015	2016	2017	2018	2019	2020	2021	2022	2023	2024	2015-2019	2015-2024
Change in Outlays	0	*	-2	-4	-9	-16	-25	-36	-49	-62	-15	-204

Notes: This option would take effect in January 2016. Estimates are relative to CBO's August 2014 baseline projections.

* = between -$500 million and zero.

The Social Security benefits that people receive in the year they are first entitled to benefits—at age 62 for retired workers and five months after the onset of disability for disabled workers—depend on a formula set in law. This option would adjust the benefit formula to reduce Social Security benefits for people who become eligible in calendar year 2016 or later. Benefits would be permanently reduced by 3 percent for people newly eligible in 2016, 6 percent for people newly eligible in 2017, and so on, up to 15 percent for people newly eligible in 2020 or later. Only future beneficiaries would be affected, so the option would not affect payments to people who turned 62 or became entitled to disability benefits before January 2016.

Option 17

Eliminate Eligibility for Starting Social Security Disability Benefits at Age 62 or Later

(Billions of dollars)	2015	2016	2017	2018	2019	2020	2021	2022	2023	2024	2015-2019	2015-2024
Change in Outlays	0	-0.1	-0.3	-0.5	-0.8	-1.1	-1.4	-1.8	-2.1	-2.5	-1.7	-10.6

Note: This option would take effect in January 2016. Estimates are relative to CBO's August 2014 baseline projections.

Under current law, people are eligible for Social Security Disability Insurance (DI) until they reach the full retirement age, which is currently 66 and is scheduled to increase gradually beginning in 2017 for those born in 1955 until it reaches 67 for workers born in 1960 or later. (All years mentioned in this option are calendar years.) Under this option, workers would not be allowed to apply for DI benefits after their 62nd birthday or to receive DI benefits if they became eligible for benefits after that date. Under such a policy, individuals who would have become eligible for DI benefits at age 62 or later under current law would instead have to claim retirement benefits if they wanted to receive any Social Security benefits. Workers who claim retirement benefits at age 62 rather than at their full retirement age receive lower benefits for as long as they live. The savings estimated from this option do not include any effects of this option on spending for other federal programs, such as Medicare, Medicaid, and the Supplemental Security Income (SSI) program.

Option 18

Require Social Security Disability Insurance Applicants to Have Worked More in Recent Years

(Billions of dollars)	2015	2016	2017	2018	2019	2020	2021	2022	2023	2024	2015-2019	2015-2024
Change in Outlays	0	-0.5	-1.2	-2.0	-2.8	-3.5	-4.4	-5.2	-6.0	-6.9	-6.4	-32.4

Note: This option would take effect in January 2016. Estimates are relative to CBO's August 2014 baseline projections.

To be eligible for benefits under Social Security Disability Insurance (DI), disabled workers must generally have worked 5 out of the past 10 years. This option would raise that threshold for recent work by requiring disabled workers older than 30 to have worked 4 of the past 6 years. The savings estimated for this option do not include any effects of this option on spending for other federal programs, such as Medicare, Medicaid, and the Supplemental Security Income (SSI) program.

Option 19

Narrow Eligibility for Veterans' Disability Compensation by Excluding Certain Disabilities Unrelated to Military Duties

(Billions of dollars)	2015	2016	2017	2018	2019	2020	2021	2022	2023	2024	2015-2019	2015-2024
Change in Outlays	0	-2.5	-2.3	-2.1	-2.3	-2.2	-2.2	-2.4	-2.2	-2.1	-9.1	-20.3

Note: This option would take effect in October 2015. Estimates are relative to CBO's August 2014 baseline projections.

Veterans may receive disability compensation from the Department of Veterans Affairs for medical conditions or injuries that occurred or worsened during active-duty military service (excluding those resulting from willful misconduct). Some medical conditions and injuries that are deemed to be service-connected disabilities were incurred or exacerbated in the performance of military duties, but others were not. According to the Government Accountability Office (GAO), seven qualifying medical conditions that are generally neither caused nor aggravated by military service are chronic obstructive

pulmonary disease, arteriosclerotic heart disease, hemorrhoids, uterine fibroids, multiple sclerosis, Crohn's disease, and osteoarthritis.

This option would cease veterans' disability compensation for the seven medical conditions identified by GAO. Under the option, veterans currently receiving compensation for those conditions would have their compensation reduced or eliminated following a reevaluation, and veterans who applied for compensation for those conditions in the future would not be eligible for it.

Option 20

Restrict VA's Individual Unemployability Benefits to Disabled Veterans Who Are Younger Than the Full Retirement Age for Social Security

(Billions of dollars)	2015	2016	2017	2018	2019	2020	2021	2022	2023	2024	2015-2019	2015-2024
Change in Outlays	0	-1.0	-1.9	-1.9	-1.9	-1.9	-1.9	-1.9	-1.9	-1.9	-6.7	-16.3

Note: This option would take effect in October 2015. Estimates are relative to CBO's August 2014 baseline projections.

The Department of Veterans Affairs (VA) supplements regular disability compensation payments with Individual Unemployability (IU) payments for low-income veterans that it deems unable to engage in substantial work. To qualify, veterans' wages or salaries cannot exceed the federal poverty guidelines for a single person, and applicants generally must be rated between 60 percent and 90 percent disabled. A veteran qualifying for the IU supplement receives a monthly disability payment equal to the

amount that he or she would receive with a 100 percent disability rating.

Under this option, VA would no longer make IU payments to veterans who were past Social Security's full retirement age, which varies from 65 to 67, depending on a beneficiary's birth year. Therefore, at the full retirement age, VA disability payments would revert to the amount associated with the disability rating.

Option 21

Use an Alternative Measure of Inflation to Index Social Security and Other Mandatory Programs

(Billions of dollars)	2015	2016	2017	2018	2019	2020	2021	2022	2023	2024	2015-2019	2015-2024
Change in Outlays												
Social Security	0	-1.7	-4.1	-6.7	-9.5	-12.5	-15.7	-18.9	-22.1	-25.2	-22.0	-116.4
Other benefit programs with COLAs[a]	0	-0.6	-1.3	-1.9	-2.7	-3.4	-4.2	-5.2	-5.7	-6.0	-6.4	-31.0
Effects on SNAP from interactions with COLA programs[b]	0	*	0.1	0.1	0.2	0.3	0.3	0.4	0.4	0.5	0.5	2.3
Health programs	0	-0.5	-1.0	-1.5	-2.2	-3.3	-4.2	-5.0	-6.8	-7.3	-5.2	-31.8
Other federal spending[c]	0	*	-0.2	-0.4	-0.4	-0.5	-0.6	-0.7	-0.8	-1.1	-1.0	-4.8
Total	0	-2.8	-6.5	-10.3	-14.6	-19.5	-24.3	-29.4	-35.0	-39.2	-34.2	-181.7
Change in Revenues[d]	0	*	*	*	*	*	*	*	*	*	*	-0.1
Net Effect on the Deficit	0	-2.9	-6.5	-10.3	-14.6	-19.5	-24.3	-29.4	-35.0	-39.2	-34.2	-181.6

Sources: Congressional Budget Office; staff of the Joint Committee on Taxation.

Notes: This option would take effect in January 2016. Estimates are relative to CBO's August 2014 baseline projections.

This estimate does not include the effects of using the chained consumer price index for parameters in the tax code.

COLA = cost-of-living adjustment; SNAP = Supplemental Nutrition Assistance Program; * = between -$50 million and $50 million.

a. Other benefit programs with COLAs include civil service retirement, military retirement, Supplemental Security Income, veterans' pensions and compensation, and other retirement programs whose COLAs are linked directly to those for Social Security or civil service retirement.

b. The policy change would reduce payments from other federal programs to people who also receive benefits from SNAP. Because SNAP benefits are based on a formula that considers such income, a decrease in those other payments would lead to an increase in SNAP benefits.

c. Other federal spending includes changes to benefits and various aspects (eligibility thresholds, funding levels, and payment rates, for instance) of other federal programs, such as those providing Pell grants and student loans, SNAP, child nutrition programs, and programs (other than health programs) linked to the federal poverty guidelines. (The changes in spending on SNAP included here are those besides the changes in benefits that result from interactions with COLA programs.)

d. The effects on revenues include changes in the revenue portion of refundable tax credits for health insurance purchased through exchanges, as well as other effects on revenues of the Affordable Care Act's provisions related to insurance coverage.

Cost-of-living adjustments (COLAs) for Social Security and many other parameters of federal programs are currently indexed to increases in the consumer price index (CPI), a measure of overall inflation calculated by the Bureau of Labor Statistics. That agency computes another measure of inflation—the chained CPI—that is designed to account fully for changes in spending patterns and that effectively eliminates a statistical bias that exists in the traditional CPI. This option would use the chained CPI for indexing COLAs for Social Security and parameters of other programs beginning in calendar year 2016. The chained CPI has grown an average of about 0.25 percentage points more slowly per year over the past decade than the traditional CPI has, and the Congressional Budget Office expects that gap to persist. Therefore, the option would reduce federal spending, and savings would grow each year as the effects of the change compounded.

CHAPTER 3

Discretionary Spending

Option 22

Cap Increases in Basic Pay for Military Service Members

(Billions of dollars)	2015	2016	2017	2018	2019	2020	2021	2022	2023	2024	2015-2019	2015-2024
Change in Spending												
Budget authority	0	-0.4	-0.9	-1.4	-2.0	-2.5	-3.2	-3.9	-4.6	-5.3	-4.6	-24.1
Outlays	0	-0.3	-0.8	-1.4	-1.9	-2.5	-3.2	-3.8	-4.5	-5.3	-4.5	-23.8

Note: This option would take effect in January 2016. Estimates are relative to CBO's August 2014 baseline projections. About 30 percent of the savings would be reductions in intragovernmental payments and thus would not reduce the deficit.

Starting in January 2016, this option would cap basic pay, which accounts for about 70 percent of cash compensation for active duty military personnel, to increases of 0.5 percentage points below the percentage increase in the employment cost index (ECI). Use of the ECI is the default for military pay raises under current law.

Option 23

Replace Some Military Personnel With Civilian Employees

(Billions of dollars)	2015	2016	2017	2018	2019	2020	2021	2022	2023	2024	2015-2019	2015-2024
Change in Spending												
Budget authority	0	-0.3	-0.9	-1.6	-2.4	-2.9	-3.0	-3.1	-3.2	-3.3	-5.1	-20.6
Outlays	0	-0.2	-0.8	-1.4	-2.2	-2.7	-2.9	-3.0	-3.1	-3.2	-4.7	-19.7

Note: This option would take effect in October 2015. Estimates are relative to CBO's August 2014 baseline projections. About 30 percent of the savings would be reductions in intragovernmental payments and thus would not reduce the deficit.

According to data from the Department of Defense (DoD), thousands of members of the military work in support roles or in "commercial" jobs that could be performed by civilians. Under this option, over four years, DoD would replace 80,000 of the more than 500,000 uniformed military personnel in commercial jobs with 53,000 civilian employees and, as a result, decrease military end strength (the number of military personnel on the rolls as of the final day of a fiscal year) by 80,000. Those changes would reduce the need for appropriations primarily because fewer civilians would replace a given number of military personnel. (Civilians have fewer collateral duties and do not generally rotate among positions as rapidly as military personnel do.)

Option 24

Replace the Joint Strike Fighter Program With F-16s and F/A-18s

(Billions of dollars)	2015	2016	2017	2018	2019	2020	2021	2022	2023	2024	2015-2019	2015-2024
Change in Spending												
Budget authority	0	-4.9	-4.7	-4.9	-5.0	-3.5	-4.7	-4.4	-4.5	-4.4	-19.5	-41.0
Outlays	0	-1.0	-2.1	-3.0	-3.8	-4.2	-4.4	-4.3	-4.3	-4.3	-9.9	-31.4

Note: This option would take effect in October 2015. Estimates of savings displayed in the table are based on the fiscal year 2015 Future Years Defense Program and the Congressional Budget Office's extension of that program.

The Department of Defense (DoD) has ordered 179 F-35 Joint Strike Fighters and plans to purchase 2,264 more. Under this option, DoD would cancel the F-35 program and instead purchase the most advanced versions of fighter aircraft already in service. The Air Force would acquire 1,763 Lockheed Martin F-16s, and the Navy and Marine Corps would buy 680 Boeing F/A-18s.

Option 25

Stop Building Ford Class Aircraft Carriers

(Billions of dollars)	2015	2016	2017	2018	2019	2020	2021	2022	2023	2024	2015-2019	2015-2024
Change in Spending												
Budget authority	0	-0.7	-1.0	-0.8	-1.9	-2.4	-3.1	-3.9	-3.7	-2.2	-4.5	-19.9
Outlays	0	-0.1	-0.3	-0.5	-0.7	-1.1	-1.5	-2.1	-2.7	-2.9	-1.5	-11.8

Note: This option would take effect in October 2015. Estimates of savings displayed in the table are based on the fiscal year 2015 Future Years Defense Program and the Congressional Budget Office's extension of that program.

Under this option, the Navy would stop building new aircraft carriers after completion of the U.S.S. *John F. Kennedy*, which lawmakers authorized in 2013. (All years mentioned in this option are fiscal years.) Thus, the next two aircraft carriers the Navy intends to purchase under its shipbuilding plan, the U.S.S. *Enterprise* in 2018 and another carrier in 2023, would be canceled.

Option 26

Reduce the Number of Ballistic Missile Submarines

(Billions of dollars)	2015	2016	2017	2018	2019	2020	2021	2022	2023	2024	2015-2019	2015-2024
Change in Spending												
Budget authority	0	0.1	-0.8	-0.9	-3.1	-3.2	-4.7	-6.4	0.2	-2.2	-4.6	-20.9
Outlays	0	*	-0.1	-0.3	-0.8	-1.5	-2.2	-3.2	-3.6	-3.1	-1.3	-14.9

Notes: This option would take effect in October 2015. Estimates of savings displayed in the table are based on the fiscal year 2015 Future Years Defense Program and the Congressional Budget Office's extension of that program.

   * = between -$50 million and zero.

The Navy maintains a force of 14 Ohio class ballistic missile submarines (SSBNs). Over the next two decades, the Ohio class submarines will reach the end of their service life. This option would reduce the Navy's SSBN force to eight submarines in 2021 by retiring one Ohio class submarine a year over the 2016–2021 period. (All years mentioned in this option are fiscal years.) That number would be maintained after 2021 by delaying the start of the Ohio Replacement program from 2021 to 2025 and reducing the number of SSBNs purchased under that program.

Option 27

Defer Development of a New Long-Range Bomber

(Billions of dollars)	2015	2016	2017	2018	2019	2020	2021	2022	2023	2024	2015-2019	2015-2024
Change in Spending												
Budget authority	0	-1.6	-2.4	-3.1	-3.6	-5.4	-5.0	-5.1	-4.2	-3.8	-10.7	-34.2
Outlays	0	-0.9	-1.8	-2.6	-3.2	-3.6	-3.5	-3.4	-3.5	-3.7	-8.5	-26.2

Note: This option would take effect in October 2015. Estimates of savings displayed in the table are based on the fiscal year 2015 Future Years Defense Program and the Congressional Budget Office's extension of that program.

This option would defer until at least fiscal year 2025 the Air Force's program to develop a new bomber to augment and eventually replace its current fleet of 159 long-range bombers.

Option 28

Reduce Funding for International Affairs Programs

(Billions of dollars)	2015	2016	2017	2018	2019	2020	2021	2022	2023	2024	2015-2019	2015-2024
Change in Spending												
Budget authority	0	-13	-14	-14	-14	-15	-15	-15	-16	-16	-55	-131
Outlays	0	-5	-9	-11	-12	-13	-14	-14	-15	-15	-38	-109

Note: This option would take effect in October 2015. Estimates are relative to CBO's August 2014 baseline projections.

The budget for international affairs funds diplomatic and consular programs, global health initiatives, security assis- tance, and other programs. This option would reduce the total international affairs budget by 25 percent.

Option 29

Eliminate Human Space Exploration Programs

(Billions of dollars)	2015	2016	2017	2018	2019	2020	2021	2022	2023	2024	2015-2019	2015-2024
Change in Spending												
Budget authority	0	-8.2	-8.4	-8.6	-8.8	-8.9	-9.1	-9.3	-9.6	-9.8	-33.9	-80.7
Outlays	0	-5.5	-8.1	-8.4	-8.6	-8.9	-9.1	-9.3	-9.5	-9.7	-30.6	-76.9

Note: This option would take effect in October 2015. Estimates are relative to CBO's August 2014 baseline projections.

The National Aeronautics and Space Administration's (NASA's) Human Exploration and Operations programs focus on developing systems and capabilities required to explore deep space while continuing operations in low-Earth orbit. This option would terminate those programs except for the parts necessary to meet space communications needs. The agency's science and aero- nautics programs and robotic space missions would continue.

Option 30

Reduce Department of Energy Funding for Energy Technology Development

(Billions of dollars)	2015	2016	2017	2018	2019	2020	2021	2022	2023	2024	2015-2019	2015-2024
Reduce Funding for Fossil Energy Research, Development, and Demonstration												
Change in Spending												
Budget authority	0	-0.1	-0.1	-0.2	-0.2	-0.2	-0.2	-0.2	-0.2	-0.2	-0.5	-1.5
Outlays	0	*	*	-0.1	-0.1	-0.2	-0.2	-0.2	-0.2	-0.2	-0.3	-1.1
Reduce Funding for Nuclear Energy Research, Development, and Demonstration												
Change in Spending												
Budget authority	0	-0.1	-0.3	-0.5	-0.5	-0.5	-0.5	-0.5	-0.5	-0.5	-1.4	-3.8
Outlays	0	-0.1	-0.2	-0.3	-0.4	-0.5	-0.5	-0.5	-0.5	-0.5	-1.1	-3.5
Reduce Funding for Energy Efficiency and Renewable Energy Research, Development, and Demonstration												
Change in Spending												
Budget authority	0	-0.3	-0.6	-0.9	-0.9	-0.9	-0.9	-1.0	-1.0	-1.0	-2.7	-7.5
Outlays	0	-0.1	-0.2	-0.4	-0.6	-0.7	-0.8	-0.9	-0.9	-1.0	-1.4	-5.6
Total												
Change in Spending												
Budget authority	0	-0.5	-1.0	-1.5	-1.6	-1.6	-1.6	-1.7	-1.7	-1.7	-4.5	-12.8
Outlays	0	-0.2	-0.5	-0.9	-1.1	-1.3	-1.4	-1.5	-1.6	-1.7	-2.7	-10.2

Notes: This option would take effect in October 2015. Estimates are relative to CBO's August 2014 baseline projections.

    * = between -$50 million and zero.

Various programs of the Department of Energy support applied research and development and commercial demonstration of new technologies in the areas of fossil fuels, nuclear power, and energy efficiency and renewable energy. This option would reduce spending for those activities to 25 percent of their fiscal year 2014 amounts stepwise over three years. (Basic research in those areas would be exempt from those reductions.)

Option 31

Eliminate Certain Forest Service Programs

(Billions of dollars)	2015	2016	2017	2018	2019	2020	2021	2022	2023	2024	2015-2019	2015-2024
Change in Spending												
Budget authority	0	-0.6	-0.6	-0.6	-0.6	-0.6	-0.6	-0.7	-0.7	-0.7	-2.3	-5.6
Outlays	0	-0.3	-0.5	-0.5	-0.6	-0.6	-0.6	-0.6	-0.7	-0.7	-1.9	-5.2

Note: This option would take effect in October 2015. Estimates are relative to CBO's August 2014 baseline projections.

The Forest Service carries out several programs devoted to research on forestry and rangeland. This option would eliminate two of those programs—Forest and Rangeland Research and State and Private Forestry.

Option 32

Eliminate the International Trade Administration's Trade Promotion Activities

(Billions of dollars)	2015	2016	2017	2018	2019	2020	2021	2022	2023	2024	2015-2019	2015-2024
Change in Spending												
Budget authority	0	-0.3	-0.4	-0.4	-0.4	-0.4	-0.4	-0.4	-0.4	-0.4	-1.4	-3.5
Outlays	0	-0.3	-0.3	-0.4	-0.4	-0.4	-0.4	-0.4	-0.4	-0.4	-1.4	-3.4

Note: This option would take effect in October 2015. Estimates are relative to CBO's August 2014 baseline projections.

The International Trade Administration (ITA) within the Department of Commerce provides support to U.S. businesses selling their goods and services abroad. ITA is one of several federal agencies that engage in trade development and promotion; it receives the largest discretionary appropriations for that purpose. This option would eliminate ITA's trade promotion activities.

Option 33

Limit Highway Funding to Expected Highway Revenues

(Billions of dollars)	2015	2016	2017	2018	2019	2020	2021	2022	2023	2024	2015-2019	2015-2024
Change in Spending												
Obligation limitations	0	-9	-9	-10	-11	-12	-13	-13	-14	-15	-39	-106
Outlays	0	-2	-6	-8	-9	-10	-11	-11	-12	-13	-24	-82

Note: This option would take effect in October 2015. Estimates are relative to CBO's August 2014 baseline projections. Most of the outlays for the highway program are controlled by limitations on obligations set in annual appropriation acts rather than by contract authority (a mandatory form of budget authority) set in authorizing law. By CBO's estimate, $685 million in contract authority is exempt from the limitations each year; spending stemming from that authority would not be affected by this option.

The last extension of the authorization for the highway program—the Highway Transportation Funding Act of 2014—provides highway funding through May 31, 2015. This option would reduce federal funding for the highway system, starting in fiscal year 2016, by lowering the obligation limitations for the Federal-Aid Highway program to the amount of projected revenues going to the highway account of the Highway Trust Fund. The federal taxes that directly fund the Highway Trust Fund would not change.

Option 34

Eliminate Grants to Large and Medium-Sized Airports

(Billions of dollars)	2015	2016	2017	2018	2019	2020	2021	2022	2023	2024	2015-2019	2015-2024
Change in Spending												
Obligation limitations	0	-1.0	-1.0	-1.0	-1.1	-1.1	-1.1	-1.1	-1.1	-1.2	-4.1	-9.7
Outlays	0	-0.2	-0.6	-0.8	-1.0	-1.0	-1.1	-1.1	-1.1	-1.1	-2.6	-8.0

Note: This option would take effect in October 2015. Estimates are relative to CBO's August 2014 baseline projections. Outlays for grants to airports are controlled by limitations on obligations set in annual appropriation acts rather than by contract authority (a mandatory form of budget authority) set in authorizing law. For the above estimates, the contract authority is assumed to equal the obligation limitations that would be in effect under the option.

Under the Airport Improvement Program (AIP), the Federal Aviation Administration provides grants to airports to expand runways, improve safety and security, and make other capital investments. In fiscal year 2013, about 30 percent of that money went to airports that are classified, on the basis of the number of passenger boardings, as large and medium-sized. This option would eliminate the AIP's grants to those airports but would continue to provide grants to smaller airports in amounts that match funding in fiscal year 2013.

Option 35

Eliminate Subsidies for Amtrak

(Billions of dollars)	2015	2016	2017	2018	2019	2020	2021	2022	2023	2024	2015-2019	2015-2024
Change in Spending												
Budget authority	0	-1.4	-1.5	-1.5	-1.5	-1.6	-1.6	-1.6	-1.6	-1.7	-7.5	-14.0
Outlays	0	-1.1	-1.3	-1.5	-1.5	-1.5	-1.6	-1.6	-1.6	-1.7	-7.0	-13.5

Note: This option would take effect in October 2015. Estimates are relative to CBO's August 2014 baseline projections.

The government covers almost all of the capital costs for passenger rail services provided by the National Railroad Passenger Corporation (or Amtrak) as well as more than 10 percent of its operating costs. This option would eliminate those subsidies.

Option 36

Eliminate Capital Investment Grants for Transit Systems

(Billions of dollars)	2015	2016	2017	2018	2019	2020	2021	2022	2023	2024	2015-2019	2015-2024
Change in Spending												
Budget authority	0	-2.0	-2.0	-2.1	-2.1	-2.2	-2.2	-2.2	-2.3	-2.3	-10.4	-19.5
Outlays	0	-0.3	-0.9	-1.3	-1.6	-1.9	-2.1	-2.1	-2.2	-2.2	-6.1	-14.7

Note: This option would take effect in October 2015. Estimates are relative to CBO's August 2014 baseline projections.

This option would eliminate the Capital Investment Grants program, which awards grants on a competitive basis to public transit systems (rail systems, bus systems that use exclusive or controlled rights-of-way, and ferries).

Option 37

Restrict Pell Grants to the Neediest Students

(Billions of dollars)	2015	2016	2017	2018	2019	2020	2021	2022	2023	2024	2015-2019	2015-2024
	Restrict Pell Grants to Students With an EFC of $3,850 or Less											
Change in Discretionary Spending												
Budget authority	-0.1	-0.1	-0.1	-0.1	-0.1	-0.1	-0.1	-0.1	-0.1	-0.1	-0.6	-1.3
Outlays	*	-0.1	-0.1	-0.1	-0.1	-0.1	-0.1	-0.1	-0.1	-0.1	-0.5	-1.2
Change in Mandatory Outlays	-0.1	-0.3	-0.4	-0.5	-0.5	-0.5	-0.5	-0.6	-0.6	-0.6	-1.7	-4.6
	Restrict Pell Grants to Students With an EFC of Zero											
Change in Discretionary Spending												
Budget authority	-6.9	-6.9	-6.9	-6.9	-6.9	-7.0	-7.0	-7.1	-7.2	-7.2	-34.5	-70.0
Outlays	-1.9	-6.9	-6.9	-6.9	-6.9	-6.9	-7.0	-7.0	-7.2	-7.2	-29.4	-64.7
Change in Mandatory Outlays	-0.6	-2.4	-2.8	-3.0	-3.1	-3.1	-3.2	-3.2	-3.3	-3.3	-12.0	-28.0

Notes: This option would take effect in July 2015. Estimates are relative to CBO's August 2014 baseline projections.

EFC = expected family contribution; * = between -$50 million and zero.

Under current law, Pell grant recipients with an expected family contribution (EFC) exceeding 90 percent of the total maximum Pell grant award (that is, an EFC greater than $5,157 for academic year 2014–2015) are ineligible for a grant. One version of this option would make students with an EFC exceeding $3,850—the eligibility ceiling in the academic year 2006–2007—ineligible for a Pell grant; that ceiling would be adjusted for inflation in subsequent years. A stricter version of this option would reduce the eligibility ceiling to an EFC of zero.

Option 38

Eliminate Federal Funding for National Community Service and Senior Community Service Employment Programs

(Billions of dollars)	2015	2016	2017	2018	2019	2020	2021	2022	2023	2024	2015-2019	2015-2024
Change in Spending												
Budget authority	0	-1.5	-1.6	-1.6	-1.6	-1.7	-1.7	-1.7	-1.8	-1.8	-6.3	-14.9
Outlays	0	-0.3	-1.1	-1.3	-1.4	-1.5	-1.5	-1.6	-1.7	-1.7	-4.1	-12.1

Note: This option would take effect in October 2015. Estimates are relative to CBO's August 2014 baseline projections.

The National Community Service and Senior Community Service Employment programs provide financial and in-kind assistance to students, seniors, and others who volunteer in their communities in areas such as education, public safety, the environment, and health care. This option would eliminate federal funding for those programs.

Option 39

Reduce Federal Funding for the Arts and Humanities

(Billions of dollars)	2015	2016	2017	2018	2019	2020	2021	2022	2023	2024	2015-2019	2015-2024
Change in Spending												
Budget authority	0	-0.4	-0.5	-0.5	-0.6	-0.6	-0.7	-0.8	-0.8	-0.9	-2.1	-5.9
Outlays	0	-0.3	-0.4	-0.5	-0.6	-0.6	-0.7	-0.7	-0.8	-0.8	-1.9	-5.5

Note: This option would take effect in October 2015. Estimates are relative to CBO's August 2014 baseline projections.

Federal funding for arts and humanities programs includes payments to the Smithsonian Institution, the Corporation for Public Broadcasting, the National Endowment for the Humanities, the National Endowment for the Arts, the National Gallery of Art, the United States Holocaust Memorial Museum, the John F. Kennedy Center for the Performing Arts, and the National Capital Arts and Cultural Affairs program. This option would cut federal support for those programs by 25 percent and would not adjust future appropriations for inflation.

Option 40

Increase Payments by Tenants in Federally Assisted Housing

(Billions of dollars)	2015	2016	2017	2018	2019	2020	2021	2022	2023	2024	2015-2019	2015-2024
Change in Spending												
Budget authority	0	-0.5	-1.0	-1.6	-2.2	-2.8	-2.9	-3.0	-3.1	-3.1	-5.3	-20.3
Outlays	0	-0.3	-0.8	-1.3	-1.9	-2.5	-2.9	-2.9	-3.0	-3.1	-4.3	-18.8

Note: This option would take effect in October 2015. Estimates are relative to CBO's August 2014 baseline projections.

Generally, low-income tenants who receive federal rental assistance must pay 30 percent of their gross family income (after certain adjustments) for rent; the federal government pays the difference between that amount and the maximum allowable rent. Under this option, tenants' rental contributions would gradually increase from 30 percent of adjusted gross family income to 35 percent over the period from fiscal years 2016 through 2020 and then remain at the higher rate.

Option 41

Reduce the Annual Across-the-Board Adjustment for Federal Civilian Employees' Pay

(Billions of dollars)	2015	2016	2017	2018	2019	2020	2021	2022	2023	2024	2015-2019	2015-2024
Change in Spending												
Budget authority	0	-0.8	-1.9	-3.1	-4.4	-5.7	-7.2	-8.7	-10.3	-12.0	-10.2	-54.0
Outlays	0	-0.8	-1.9	-3.1	-4.3	-5.7	-7.1	-8.6	-10.2	-11.9	-10.0	-53.6

Note: This option would take effect in January 2016. Estimates are relative to CBO's August 2014 baseline projections. About one-fifth of the savings would be reductions in intragovernmental payments and thus would not reduce the deficit.

Under the Federal Employees Pay Comparability Act of 1990, most federal civilian employees receive a pay adjustment each January. As specified by that law, the size of the adjustment is set at the annual rate of increase of the employment cost index (ECI) for wages and salaries in private industry minus 0.5 percentage points. Under this option, the annual across-the-board increase would be reduced by 0.5 percentage points each year from fiscal year 2016 through 2024.

Option 42

Reduce the Size of the Federal Workforce Through Attrition

(Billions of dollars)	2015	2016	2017	2018	2019	2020	2021	2022	2023	2024	2015-2019	2015-2024
Change in Spending												
Budget authority	0	-1.2	-3.5	-5.1	-5.9	-6.3	-6.6	-6.8	-7.0	-7.3	-15.6	-49.7
Outlays	0	-1.1	-3.4	-5.0	-5.9	-6.3	-6.6	-6.8	-7.0	-7.3	-15.4	-49.4

Note: This option would take effect in October 2015. Estimates are relative to CBO's August 2014 baseline projections. About one-fifth of the savings would be reductions in intragovernmental payments and thus would not reduce the deficit.

In fiscal year 2013, the federal government employed about 2.1 million civilian workers, excluding Postal Service employees. The largest costs the federal government incurred for those employees were for salaries, health insurance, and pension benefits.

This option would reduce the number of federal civilian employees at certain agencies by 10 percent by allowing those agencies to hire no more than one employee for every three workers who left. The President would be allowed to exempt an agency under certain conditions. About two-thirds of the federal civilian workforce would be exempt, the Congressional Budget Office estimates, thus limiting the workforce reduction to about 70,000 employees. (Agencies would not be allowed to hire contractors to offset the reduction in the federal workforce.)

Option 43

Impose Fees to Cover the Cost of Government Regulations and Charge for Services Provided to the Private Sector

(Billions of dollars)	2015	2016	2017	2018	2019	2020	2021	2022	2023	2024	2015-2019	2015-2024
Change in Spending												
Budget authority	0	-1.5	-1.8	-2.0	-2.3	-2.5	-2.6	-2.7	-2.7	-2.8	-7.7	-20.9
Outlays	0	-1.5	-1.8	-2.0	-2.3	-2.5	-2.6	-2.7	-2.7	-2.8	-7.7	-20.9

Note: This option would take effect in October 2015. Estimates are relative to CBO's August 2014 baseline projections. Fees collected under this option could be recorded in the budget as offsetting collections (discretionary), offsetting receipts (usually mandatory), or revenues, depending on the specific legislative language used to establish them.

This option would impose several relatively small fees and taxes to cover the cost to the government of administering regulations or to ensure that the government is compensated for the value of services and resources provided to the private sector. This option would increase fees for permits issued by the Army Corps of Engineers, set grazing fees for federal lands on the basis of the state-determined formulas used to set grazing fees for state-owned lands, impose fees on users of the St. Lawrence Seaway, increase fees for the use of the inland waterway system, impose fees that recover the costs of registering pesticides and new chemicals, charge fees to offset the cost of federal rail-safety activities, charge transaction fees to fund the Commodity Futures Trading Commission, assess new fees to cover the costs for the Food and Drug Administration to review advertising and promotional materials for prescription drugs and biological products, and collect new fees for activities of the Food Safety and Inspection Service.

Option 44

Repeal the Davis-Bacon Act

(Billions of dollars)	2015	2016	2017	2018	2019	2020	2021	2022	2023	2024	2015-2019	2015-2024
Change in Spending												
Spending authority	0	-1.5	-1.5	-1.5	-1.6	-1.6	-1.6	-1.7	-1.7	-1.7	-6.1	-14.5
Budget authority	0	-0.7	-0.8	-0.8	-0.8	-0.8	-0.8	-0.8	-0.8	-0.9	-3.0	-7.1
Outlays	0	-0.4	-0.9	-1.2	-1.4	-1.5	-1.5	-1.6	-1.6	-1.6	-3.9	-11.7

Note: This option would take effect in October 2015. Estimates are relative to CBO's August 2014 baseline projections. Spending authority includes budget authority as well as obligation limitations (such as for certain transportation programs). The option would also result in reductions in mandatory spending of less than $50 million per year (not shown in the table).

The Davis-Bacon Act requires that workers on all federally funded or federally assisted construction projects whose contracts total more than $2,000 be paid no less than "prevailing wages" in the area in which the project is located. This option would repeal the Davis-Bacon Act, which would lower the federal government's costs for construction; the option would make corresponding reductions in appropriations and in limits on the government's authority to enter into obligations for certain transportation programs.

Option 45

Eliminate or Reduce Funding for Certain Grants to State and Local Governments

(Billions of dollars)	2015	2016	2017	2018	2019	2020	2021	2022	2023	2024	2015-2019	2015-2024
	Eliminate Department of Energy Grants for Energy Conservation and Weatherization											
Change in Spending												
Budget authority	0	-0.2	-0.2	-0.2	-0.3	-0.3	-0.3	-0.3	-0.3	-0.3	-1.0	-2.3
Outlays	0	-0.1	-0.1	-0.2	-0.2	-0.2	-0.2	-0.3	-0.3	-0.3	-0.6	-1.8
	Phase Out Environmental Protection Agency Grants for Wastewater and Drinking Water Infrastructure											
Change in Spending												
Budget authority	0	-0.2	-1.2	-2.5	-2.5	-2.6	-2.6	-2.7	-2.7	-2.8	-6.4	-19.8
Outlays	0	*	-0.1	-0.4	-1.1	-1.7	-2.1	-2.3	-2.4	-2.5	-1.6	-12.6
	Eliminate New Funding for Community Development Block Grants											
Change in Spending												
Budget authority	0	-3.2	-3.3	-3.3	-3.4	-3.5	-3.5	-3.6	-3.7	-3.8	-13.2	-31.3
Outlays	0	*	-0.8	-2.4	-3.1	-3.3	-3.3	-3.4	-3.5	-3.6	-6.2	-23.3
	Eliminate Certain Department of Education Grants											
Change in Spending												
Budget authority	0	-1.5	-1.5	-1.5	-1.6	-1.6	-1.6	-1.7	-1.7	-1.7	-6.1	-14.3
Outlays	0	*	-0.9	-1.3	-1.5	-1.5	-1.6	-1.6	-1.6	-1.7	-3.8	-11.8
	Decrease Funding for Certain Department of Justice Grants											
Change in Spending												
Budget authority	0	-0.5	-0.5	-0.6	-0.6	-0.6	-0.6	-0.6	-0.6	-0.6	-2.2	-5.2
Outlays	0	-0.1	-0.3	-0.4	-0.5	-0.6	-0.6	-0.6	-0.6	-0.6	-1.2	-4.1
	Total											
Change in Spending												
Budget authority	0	-5.7	-6.8	-8.1	-8.3	-8.5	-8.6	-8.8	-9.0	-9.2	-28.9	-72.9
Outlays	0	-0.2	-2.1	-4.7	-6.3	-7.3	-7.8	-8.2	-8.4	-8.6	-13.4	-53.7

Notes: This option would take effect in October 2015. Estimates are relative to CBO's August 2014 baseline projections.

    * = between -$50 million and zero.

The federal government provides a variety of grants to state and local governments. This option would eliminate new funding for the Department of Energy's grants for energy conservation and weatherization; phase out grants from the Environmental Protection Agency for wastewater and drinking water infrastructure over three years; eliminate new funding for the Community Development Block Grant program; eliminate Department of Education grants that fund nonacademic programs that address the physical, emotional, and social well-being of students; and decrease funding for certain Department of Justice grants to nonprofit community organizations and state and local law enforcement agencies by 25 percent relative to the Congressional Budget Office's baseline.

Revenues

Option 46

Increase Individual Income Tax Rates

(Billions of dollars)	2015	2016	2017	2018	2019	2020	2021	2022	2023	2024	2015- 2019	2015- 2024
Change in Revenues												
Raise all tax rates on ordinary income by 1 percentage point	39	59	62	65	68	72	75	79	83	87	293	689
Raise ordinary income tax rates in the following brackets by 1 percentage point: 28 percent and over	8	12	12	13	14	15	16	17	18	19	59	144
Raise ordinary income tax rates in the following brackets by 1 percentage point: 35 percent and over	5	7	8	8	9	10	10	11	12	12	37	91

Source: Staff of the Joint Committee on Taxation.

Note: This option would take effect in January 2015. Estimates are relative to CBO's April 2014 baseline projections. The estimates include the effects on outlays resulting from changes in refundable tax credits.

Under current law, ordinary income earned by most individuals is taxed at the following seven statutory rates: 10 percent, 15 percent, 25 percent, 28 percent, 33 percent, 35 percent, and 39.6 percent. (Ordinary income is all income subject to the income tax except long-term capital gains and dividends, which are taxed under a separate rate schedule.) Some taxpayers face other statutory income tax rates. Higher-income taxpayers are subject to an additional tax of 3.8 percent on investment income, and taxpayers who are subject to the alternative minimum tax (AMT) face statutory rates of 26 percent and 28 percent. (The AMT is a parallel income tax system with fewer exemptions, deductions, credits, and rates than the regular income tax. Households must calculate the amount they owe under both the AMT and the regular income tax and pay the larger of the two amounts.)

This option includes three alternative approaches for increasing the regular statutory rates under the individual income tax. Those approaches would raise all tax rates on ordinary income (income subject to the regular rate schedule) by 1 percentage point, raise all tax rates on ordinary income in the top four brackets—28 percent and over—by 1 percentage point, and raise all tax rates on ordinary income in the top two brackets—35 percent and over—by 1 percentage point.

Option 47

Implement a New Minimum Tax on Adjusted Gross Income

(Billions of dollars)	2015	2016	2017	2018	2019	2020	2021	2022	2023	2024	2015-2019	2015-2024
Change in Revenues	0.8	5.4	5.8	6.3	7.0	7.3	7.7	8.2	8.6	9.0	25.3	66.1

Source: Staff of the Joint Committee on Taxation.

Note: This option would take effect in January 2015. Estimates are relative to CBO's April 2014 baseline projections.

Under current law, individual taxpayers are subject to statutory tax rates on ordinary income (income other than capital gains and dividends) that rise from 0 percent to 39.6 percent. Higher-income taxpayers face an additional tax of 3.8 percent on investment earnings. However, people in the highest tax brackets generally may pay a smaller share of their income in income taxes than those rates might suggest, for at least two reasons. First, income realized from capital gains and dividends—which represents a substantial share of income for many people in the highest brackets—is generally subject to lower income tax rates. Second, taxpayers can claim exemptions and deductions to reduce their taxable income, and they can further lower their tax liability using credits.

This option would impose a new minimum tax equal to 30 percent of adjusted gross income, or AGI. (AGI includes income from all sources not specifically excluded by the tax code, minus certain deductions.) To reduce the liability associated with the new minimum tax, taxpayers could use just one credit equal to 28 percent of their charitable contributions. Taxpayers would pay whichever was higher: the new minimum tax or the sum of individual income taxes owed by the taxpayer and the portion of payroll taxes he or she paid as an employee. The new minimum tax would be phased in for taxpayers with AGI between $1 million and $2 million beginning in calendar year 2015; those thresholds would be adjusted, or indexed, for inflation thereafter.

Option 48

Raise the Tax Rates on Long-Term Capital Gains and Dividends by 2 Percentage Points

(Billions of dollars)	2015	2016	2017	2018	2019	2020	2021	2022	2023	2024	2015-2019	2015-2024
Change in Revenues	1.3	4.9	5.1	5.3	5.5	5.8	5.9	6.2	6.4	6.6	22.1	52.9

Source: Staff of the Joint Committee on Taxation.

Note: This option would take effect in January 2015. Estimates are relative to CBO's April 2014 baseline projections.

When individuals sell an asset for more than the price at which they obtained it, they generally realize a capital gain that is subject to taxation. Long-term gains (those realized on assets held for more than a year) and qualified dividends (generally paid by domestic corporations or certain foreign corporations) are taxed at lower rates than taxpayers' ordinary income—that is, income from other sources, such as wages, interest, and nonqualified dividends.

This option would raise the basic tax rates on long-term capital gains and qualified dividends by 2 percentage points. Those basic rates would then be 2 percent for taxpayers in the 10 percent and 15 percent brackets for ordinary income, 17 percent for taxpayers in the brackets ranging from 25 percent through 35 percent, and 22 percent for taxpayers in the top bracket. The option would not change the other provisions of the tax code that also affect taxes on capital gains and dividends.

Option 49

Use an Alternative Measure of Inflation to Index Some Parameters of the Tax Code

(Billions of dollars)	2015	2016	2017	2018	2019	2020	2021	2022	2023	2024	2015-2019	2015-2024
Change in Revenues	1	5	7	8	11	16	20	23	27	32	33	150

Source: Staff of the Joint Committee on Taxation.

Note: This option would take effect in January 2015. Estimates are relative to CBO's April 2014 baseline projections. The estimates include the effects on outlays resulting from changes in refundable tax credits.

Some parameters of the tax code are adjusted each year on the basis of changes in the prices of goods and services, as measured by the consumer price index for all urban consumers (CPI-U), to keep their values relatively stable in real (inflation-adjusted) terms. Under this option, the chained CPI-U would be used instead of the standard CPI-U to adjust various parameters of the tax code. The Congressional Budget Office estimates that the chained CPI-U is likely to grow at an average annual rate that is 0.25 percentage points less than growth in the standard CPI-U over the next decade. Therefore, using the chained CPI-U to index tax parameters would increase the amount of income subject to taxation and result in higher tax revenues.

Option 50

Convert the Mortgage Interest Deduction to a 15 Percent Tax Credit

(Billions of dollars)	2015	2016	2017	2018	2019	2020	2021	2022	2023	2024	2015-2019	2015-2024
Change in Revenues	*	1	2	3	4	10	21	23	24	26	9	113

Source: Staff of the Joint Committee on Taxation.

Notes: This option would take effect in January 2015. Estimates are relative to CBO's April 2014 baseline projections. The estimates include the effects on outlays resulting from changes in refundable tax credits.

* = between zero and $500 million.

Homeowners can deduct mortgage interest and property taxes from their income if they itemize deductions. Under current law, the tax code limits the amount of mortgage debt that can be included in calculating the interest deduction to $1.1 million: $1 million for debt that a homeowner incurs to buy, build, or improve a first or second home; and $100,000 for other debt (such as a home-equity loan) for which the owner uses the personal residence as security, regardless of the purpose of that loan.

This option would gradually convert the tax deduction for mortgage interest to a 15 percent nonrefundable tax credit. The option would be phased in over six years, beginning in 2015. (All years referred to in this option are calendar years.) From 2015 through 2019, the deduction would still be available, but the maximum amount of the mortgage deduction would be reduced by $100,000 each year—to $1 million in 2015, $900,000 in 2016, and so on, until it reached $600,000 in 2019. In 2020 and later years, the deduction would be replaced by a 15 percent credit, the maximum amount of mortgage debt that could be included in the credit calculation would be $500,000, and the credit could be applied only to interest on debt incurred to buy, build, or improve a first home. (Other types of loans, such as those incurred to buy second homes and those using homes as security, would be excluded.) Because the credit would be nonrefundable, people with no income tax liability before the credit was taken into account would not receive any credit, and people whose precredit income tax liability was less than the full amount of the credit would receive only the portion of the credit that offsets the amount of taxes they otherwise would owe. The maximum amount that could be included in the credit calculation would not be adjusted for inflation after 2020.

Option 51

Eliminate the Deduction for State and Local Taxes

(Billions of dollars)	2015	2016	2017	2018	2019	2020	2021	2022	2023	2024	2015-2019	2015-2024
Change in Revenues	25	101	100	106	112	117	122	129	135	142	445	1088

Source: Staff of the Joint Committee on Taxation.

Note: This option would take effect in January 2015. Estimates are relative to CBO's April 2014 baseline projections.

In determining their taxable income, taxpayers may choose the standard deduction when they file their tax returns, or they may itemize and deduct certain expenses (including state and local taxes on income, real estate, and personal property) from their adjusted gross income, or AGI. (AGI includes income from all sources not specifically excluded by the tax code, minus certain deductions.) The total value of certain itemized deductions—including the deduction for state and local taxes—is reduced if the taxpayer's AGI is above a specified threshold. This option would eliminate the deductibility of state and local tax payments.

Option 52

Curtail the Deduction for Charitable Giving

(Billions of dollars)	2015	2016	2017	2018	2019	2020	2021	2022	2023	2024	2015-2019	2015-2024
Change in Revenues	4	19	20	21	22	23	24	25	26	27	87	213

Source: Staff of the Joint Committee on Taxation.

Note: This option would take effect in January 2015. Estimates are relative to CBO's April 2014 baseline projections.

Current law allows taxpayers who itemize to deduct the value of their contributions to qualifying charitable organizations. The deduction is restricted in two ways. First, charitable contributions may not exceed 50 percent of a taxpayer's adjusted gross income (AGI) in any one year. (AGI includes income from all sources not specifically excluded by the tax code, minus certain deductions.) Second, the total value of certain itemized deductions—including the deduction for charitable donations—is reduced if the taxpayer's AGI is above a specified threshold.

This option would further curtail the deduction for charitable donations while preserving a tax incentive for donating. Only contributions in excess of 2 percent of AGI would be deductible for a taxpayer who itemizes. That amount would still be subject to the additional reduction described above for higher-income taxpayers.

Option 53

Limit the Value of Itemized Deductions

(Billions of dollars)	2015	2016	2017	2018	2019	2020	2021	2022	2023	2024	2015-2019	2015-2024
Change in Revenues												
Limit the tax benefits of itemized deductions to 28 percent of their total value	6	12	13	14	14	15	16	16	17	18	58	139
Limit the tax value of itemized deductions to 6 percent of adjusted gross income	3	6	6	7	7	7	7	7	7	7	29	64
Limit itemized deductions to $500,000 for joint filers ($250,000 for all others)	5	10	11	11	12	12	13	13	14	14	48	113

Source: Staff of the Joint Committee on Taxation.

Note: This option would take effect in January 2015. Estimates are relative to CBO's April 2014 baseline projections.

When preparing their income tax returns, taxpayers may either choose the standard deduction—which is a flat dollar amount—or choose to itemize and deduct certain expenses, such as state and local taxes, mortgage interest, charitable contributions, and some medical expenses. The tax code imposes some limits on the amount of itemized deductions that taxpayers can claim. For example, the total value of certain itemized deductions is generally reduced by 3 percent of the amount by which a taxpayer's adjusted gross income exceeds a specified threshold. (Adjusted gross income includes income from all sources not specifically excluded by the tax code, minus certain deductions.) That limit, originally proposed by Congressman Donald Pease, is often called the Pease limitation.

This option considers three alternative approaches that would replace the Pease limitation with broader restrictions on the total amount of itemized deductions that taxpayers are allowed to take. The first alternative would limit the tax benefits of itemized deductions to 28 percent of the deductions' total value. The second alternative would limit the tax benefits of itemized deductions to 6 percent of a taxpayer's adjusted gross income. The third alternative would limit itemized deductions to $500,000 for married taxpayers who file joint returns and $250,000 for other taxpayers, with those thresholds adjusted, or indexed, for inflation.

Option 54

Include All Income That U.S. Citizens Earn Abroad in Taxable Income

(Billions of dollars)	2015	2016	2017	2018	2019	2020	2021	2022	2023	2024	2015-2019	2015-2024
Change in Revenues	3.9	8.0	8.4	8.9	9.4	10.1	10.7	11.4	12.2	13.2	38.6	96.2

Source: Staff of the Joint Committee on Taxation.

Note: This option would take effect in January 2015. Estimates are relative to CBO's April 2014 baseline projections. The estimates include the effects on outlays resulting from changes in refundable tax credits.

U.S. citizens who live in other countries must file an individual U.S. tax return each year, but several provisions of the tax code reduce their U.S. tax liability. First, those citizens may exclude from taxation some of the income they earn abroad: up to $99,200 for single filers and up to $198,400 for joint filers in calendar year 2014. (Those amounts are adjusted, or indexed, for inflation.) Second, under certain circumstances, U.S. citizens living abroad can also claim an exclusion or deduction for any allowance their employers provide for housing in a foreign country. Those two tax provisions—combined with the personal exemptions and deductions available to taxpayers living in either the United States or other countries—mean that U.S. citizens who reside abroad and earn over $100,000 (or, in the case of married U.S. citizens living abroad, over $200,000) may not incur any U.S. income tax liability, even if they pay no taxes to the country in which they live. Third, if those citizens pay taxes to the country in which they live, they can

receive a credit on their U.S. taxes for foreign taxes paid on any income above the U.S. exclusion amount. As a result, most U.S. tax filers who live abroad do not have any U.S. tax liability.

This option would retain the credit for taxes paid to foreign governments but would require U.S. citizens living overseas to include all of the income they earned abroad, including housing allowances, in their adjusted gross income. (Adjusted gross income includes income from all sources not specifically excluded by the tax code, minus certain deductions.) As a result, U.S. citizens living in countries with lower tax rates than those in the United States would tend to owe more—in some cases, potentially much more—in U.S. taxes than under current law, while U.S. citizens residing in countries with higher tax rates would generally continue not to owe U.S. taxes on their earned income.

Option 55

Tax Social Security and Railroad Retirement Benefits in the Same Way That Distributions From Defined Benefit Pensions Are Taxed

(Billions of dollars)	2015	2016	2017	2018	2019	2020	2021	2022	2023	2024	2015- 2019	2015- 2024
Change in Revenues	17	36	37	39	41	44	46	48	51	53	171	412

Source: Staff of the Joint Committee on Taxation.

Note: This option would take effect in January 2015. Estimates are relative to CBO's April 2014 baseline projections.

Under current law, recipients of Social Security and Railroad Retirement benefits with income below a specified threshold pay no taxes on those benefits. If the sum of their adjusted gross income (excluding any Social Security benefits), their nontaxable interest income, and one-half of their Social Security and Tier I Railroad Retirement benefits exceeds that threshold, up to 50 percent of the benefits are taxed. Above a higher threshold, as much as 85 percent of the benefits are taxed. By contrast, distributions from defined benefit plans are taxable except for the portion that represents the recovery of an employee's "basis"—that is, his or her after-tax contributions to the plan.

This option would treat the Social Security and Railroad Retirement programs in the same way that defined benefit pensions are treated—by defining a basis and taxing only those benefits that exceed that amount. For employed individuals, the basis would be the payroll taxes they paid out of after-tax income to support those programs (but not the equal amount that employers paid on their workers' behalf). For self-employed people, the basis would be the portion (50 percent) of their self-employment taxes that is not deductible from their taxable income

Option 56

Further Limit Annual Contributions to Retirement Plans

(Billions of dollars)	2015	2016	2017	2018	2019	2020	2021	2022	2023	2024	2015–2019	2015–2024
Change in Revenues	4.9	7.2	7.5	8.0	8.4	8.6	8.8	9.3	9.7	10.1	36.0	82.5

Source: Staff of the Joint Committee on Taxation.

Note: This option would take effect in January 2015. Estimates are relative to CBO's April 2014 baseline projections. To the extent that the option would affect Social Security payroll taxes, a portion of the revenues would be off-budget. In addition, the option would increase outlays for Social Security by a small amount. The estimates do not include those effects on outlays.

Current law allows taxpayers to make contributions to certain types of tax-preferred retirement plans up to a maximum annual amount that varies depending on the type of plan and the age of the taxpayer. Annual contribution limits for all types of plans are adjusted, or indexed, for inflation but increase only in $500 increments. In 2014, contributions to individual retirement accounts (IRAs) are limited to $5,500 for taxpayers under the age of 50 and $6,500 for those ages 50 and above. (All years referred to in this option are calendar years.)

Individuals under the age of 50 may contribute up to $17,500 to 401(k) and similar employment-based defined contribution plans in 2014; participants ages 50 and above are also allowed to make "catch-up" contributions of up to $5,500. In general, the limits on an individual's contributions apply to all defined contribution plans combined. However, contributions to 457(b) plans, available primarily to employees of state and local governments, are subject to a separate limit. As a result, employees who are enrolled in both 401(k) and 457(b) plans can

contribute the maximum amount to both plans, thereby allowing some people to make tax-preferred contributions of as much as $46,000 in a single year. Employers may also contribute to their workers' defined contribution plans, up to a maximum of $52,000 per person in 2014, less any contributions made by the employee.

Under this option, individuals' maximum allowable contributions, regardless of a taxpayer's age, would be reduced to about 85 percent of the current-law amount that applies to individuals under the age of 50. For 2015, the limits would be $5,000 per year for IRAs and $15,500 per year for 401(k)–type plans. The option would also require that all contributions to employment-based plans—including 457(b) plans—be subject to a single combined limit. Total allowable employer and employee contributions to a defined contribution plan would be reduced from $52,000 per year to $47,000. Annual contribution limits after 2015 would continue to be adjusted for inflation.

Option 57

Eliminate the Tax Exemption for New Qualified Private Activity Bonds

(Billions of dollars)	2015	2016	2017	2018	2019	2020	2021	2022	2023	2024	2015–2019	2015–2024
Change in Revenues	0.1	0.5	1.0	1.6	2.3	3.2	4.1	5.0	5.9	6.5	5.5	30.2

Source: Staff of the Joint Committee on Taxation.

Note: This option would take effect in January 2015. Estimates are relative to CBO's April 2014 baseline projections.

The U.S. tax code permits state and local governments to finance certain projects by issuing bonds whose interest payments are generally exempt from federal income taxes. For the most part, proceeds from tax-exempt bonds finance public projects, such as the construction of schools and highways. In some cases, however, state and local governments issue tax-exempt bonds—which are

known as qualified private activity bonds—to fund private projects that provide at least some public benefits. Eligible projects include the construction or repair of infrastructure and certain activities, such as building schools and hospitals, undertaken by nonprofit organizations. This option would eliminate the tax exemption for new qualified private activity bonds.

Option 58

Eliminate Certain Tax Preferences for Education Expenses

(Billions of dollars)	2015	2016	2017	2018	2019	2020	2021	2022	2023	2024	2015-2019	2015-2024
Change in Revenues	5	24	25	22	11	12	12	13	13	14	87	150

Source: Staff of the Joint Committee on Taxation.

Note: This option would take effect in January 2015. Estimates are relative to CBO's April 2014 baseline projections. The estimates include the effects on outlays resulting from changes in refundable tax credits.

Federal support for higher education takes many forms, including grants, subsidized loans, and tax preferences. The major tax preferences in effect in 2014 (all years referred to in this option are calendar years) or scheduled to be reinstated under current law are the following:

- The American Opportunity Tax Credit (AOTC), which can total as much as $2,500 (100 percent of the first $2,000 in qualifying education expenses and then 25 percent of the next $2,000) in 2014;

- The Lifetime Learning tax credit, which provides up to $2,000 for qualifying tuition and fees;

- The Hope tax credit, which is not currently available but is scheduled to be reinstated in 2018 when the

AOTC expires and was equal to 100 percent of the first $1,200 of qualifying tuition and fees and 50 percent of the next $1,200 for a maximum credit of $1,800 per year in 2008 (the last year it was available); and

- Tax deductions of up to $2,500 per year for interest payments on student loans.

This option would eliminate the AOTC and the Lifetime Learning tax credit and cancel the reinstatement of the Hope tax credit. The option would also gradually eliminate the deductibility of interest expenses for student loans by phasing them out in annual increments of $250 over a 10-year period.

Option 59

Lower the Investment Income Limit for the Earned Income Tax Credit and Extend That Limit to the Refundable Portion of the Child Tax Credit

(Billions of dollars)	2015	2016	2017	2018	2019	2020	2021	2022	2023	2024	2015-2019	2015-2024
Change in Revenues	*	0.8	0.8	0.8	0.7	0.7	0.7	0.6	0.7	0.7	3.1	6.3

Source: Staff of the Joint Committee on Taxation.

Notes: This option would take effect in January 2015. Estimates are relative to CBO's April 2014 baseline projections. The estimates represent the change in the overall budget balance that would result from the sum of changes to revenues and outlays.

  * = between zero and $50 million.

Low- and moderate-income people are eligible for certain refundable tax credits under the individual income tax if they meet specified criteria. If the amount of a refundable tax credit exceeds a taxpayer's tax liability before that credit is applied, the government pays the excess to that person. Two refundable tax credits are available only to workers: the earned income tax credit (EITC) and the refundable portion of the child tax credit (referred to in the tax code as the additional child tax credit). Eligibility for the EITC is restricted to filers with investment income that is $3,350 or less in calendar year 2014. Investment income includes interest (counting tax-exempt interest), dividends, capital gains, royalties and rents from personal property, and returns from passive activities (business pursuits in which the person is not actively involved). The limitation on investment income is adjusted, or indexed, for inflation each year.

This option would lower the threshold for the EITC investment income test from $3,350 to $1,650. As under current law, that threshold would be indexed for inflation. Moreover, the option would extend that limitation to the refundable portion of the child tax credit.

Option 60

Increase the Maximum Taxable Earnings for the Social Security Payroll Tax

(Billions of dollars)	2015	2016	2017	2018	2019	2020	2021	2022	2023	2024	2015-2019	2015-2024
Change in Outlays	*	*	*	1	1	1	2	2	3	4	2	15
Change in Revenues	13	63	66	69	72	74	77	81	84	87	283	687
Net Effect on the Deficit	-13	-62	-66	-69	-71	-73	-76	-78	-81	-84	-280	-672

Sources: Staff of the Joint Committee on Taxation; Congressional Budget Office.

Notes: This option would take effect in January 2015. Estimates are relative to CBO's April 2014 baseline projections. The estimate includes the reduction in individual income tax revenues that would result from a shift of some labor compensation from a taxable to a nontaxable form. The change in revenues would consist of an increase in receipts from Social Security payroll taxes (which would be off-budget), offset in part by a reduction in individual income tax revenues (which would be on-budget). The outlays would be for additional payments of Social Security benefits and would be classified as off-budget.

* = between zero and $500 million.

Social Security—which consists of Old-Age and Survivors Insurance and Disability Insurance—is financed by payroll taxes on employers, employees, and the self-employed. Only earnings up to a maximum, which is $117,000 in 2014, are subject to the tax. (All years referred to in this option are calendar years.) That maximum is indexed so that it usually increases each year at the same rate as average wages in the economy.

This option would increase the taxable share of earnings from jobs covered by Social Security (which was 83 percent in 2011) to 90 percent in 2015 by raising the maximum taxable amount to $241,600. (In later years, the maximum would continue to be indexed as it is now.) Because Social Security benefits are tied to the amount of earnings on which taxes are paid, however, some of the increase in revenues from this option would be offset by additional benefits paid to people with earnings above the maximum taxable amount under current law.

Option 61

Increase the Payroll Tax Rate for Medicare Hospital Insurance by 1 Percentage Point

(Billions of dollars)	2015	2016	2017	2018	2019	2020	2021	2022	2023	2024	2015-2019	2015-2024
Change in Revenues	45	71	74	77	80	84	87	91	95	99	346	800

Source: Staff of the Joint Committee on Taxation.

Note: This option would take effect in January 2015. Estimates are relative to CBO's April 2014 baseline projections. The estimate includes the reduction in individual income tax revenues that would result from a shift of some labor compensation from a taxable to a nontaxable form.

The primary source of financing for Hospital Insurance (HI) benefits provided under Medicare Part A is the HI payroll tax. The basic HI tax is 2.9 percent of earnings: 1.45 percent is deducted from employees' paychecks, and 1.45 percent is paid by employers. Self-employed individuals generally pay 2.9 percent of their net income in HI taxes. Unlike the payroll tax for Social Security, which applies to earnings up to an annual maximum ($117,00 in calendar year 2014), the 2.9 percent HI tax is levied on total earnings.

In addition, at earnings above $200,000, the portion of the HI tax that employees pay increases by a 0.9 percentage point surtax—to a total of 2.35 percent. (For a married couple filing an income tax return jointly, the surtax applies to the couple's combined earnings above $250,000.) The surtax does not apply to the portion of the HI tax paid by employers, which remains 1.45 percent of earnings, regardless of how much the worker earns.

This option would increase the basic HI tax on total earnings by 1.0 percentage point. The basic rate for both employers and employees would increase by 0.5 percentage points, to 1.95 percent, resulting in a combined rate of 3.9 percent. The rate paid by self-employed people would also rise to 3.9 percent. For taxpayers with earnings above $200,000 ($250,000 for married couples filing jointly), the HI tax on earnings in excess of the surtax threshold would increase from 3.8 percent to 4.8 percent; employees would pay 2.85 percent, and employers would pay the remaining 1.95 percent.

Option 62

Increase Taxes That Finance the Federal Share of the Unemployment Insurance System

(Billions of dollars)	2015	2016	2017	2018	2019	2020	2021	2022	2023	2024	2015-2019	2015-2024
Change in Revenues												
Increase the net FUTA rate to 0.8 percent	1.1	1.4	1.4	1.5	1.5	1.5	1.5	1.5	1.5	1.5	6.8	14.4
Increase the FUTA base to $14,000, index the base to future wage growth, and decrease the net FUTA rate to 0.33 percent	4.0	8.2	2.5	-2.8	-0.6	-2.6	0.1	0.2	0.3	0.4	11.2	9.6

Notes: This option would take effect in January 2015. Estimates are relative to CBO's April 2014 baseline projections.

   FUTA = Federal Unemployment Tax Act.

The unemployment insurance system is a partnership between the federal government and state governments that provides a temporary weekly benefit—consisting of a regular benefit and, often during economic downturns, extended and emergency benefits—to qualified workers who lose their job through no fault of their own. Funding for the federal portion of the unemployment insurance system is drawn from payroll taxes imposed on employers under the Federal Unemployment Tax Act (FUTA). FUTA taxes are levied on each worker's wages up to $7,000 and then deposited into several federal accounts. That amount is not adjusted, or indexed, for inflation and has remained unchanged since 1983. The FUTA tax rate is 6.0 percent, reduced by a credit of 5.4 percent for state taxes paid, for a net tax rate of 0.6 percent—or $42 for each employee earning at least $7,000 annually. On January 1, 1976, a surtax of 0.2 percent went into effect,

raising the total FUTA tax rate, net of the state tax credits, to 0.8 percent—for a maximum of $56 per employee. However, that surtax expired on July 1, 2011.

This option includes two alternative approaches that would increase revenues from unemployment insurance taxes by roughly the same amount over the next decade. The first approach would leave the FUTA tax base unchanged but would raise the net FUTA tax rate by reinstating and permanently extending the 0.2 percent FUTA surtax. The second approach would expand the FUTA tax base but decrease the tax rate. Specifically, the approach would raise the amount of wages subject to the FUTA tax from $7,000 to $14,000 in 2015 (and then index that threshold to the growth in future wages), and it would reduce the net FUTA tax rate, after the 5.4 percent credit for state taxes paid, to 0.33 percent.

Option 63

Increase Corporate Income Tax Rates by 1 Percentage Point

(Billions of dollars)	2015	2016	2017	2018	2019	2020	2021	2022	2023	2024	2015-2019	2015-2024
Change in Revenues	7	10	10	10	10	10	11	11	12	12	46	102

Source: Staff of the Joint Committee on Taxation.

Note: This option would take effect in January 2015. Estimates are relative to CBO's April 2014 baseline projections.

Most corporations that are subject to the corporate income tax calculate their tax liability according to a progressive rate schedule. The first $50,000 of corporate taxable income (after deductions and exclusions) is taxed at a rate of 15 percent; income of $50,000 to $75,000 is taxed at a 25 percent rate; income of $75,000 to $10 million is taxed at a 34 percent rate; and income above $10 million is generally taxed at a rate of 35 percent. Although most corporate taxable income falls within the 35 percent tax bracket, the average tax rate (corporate taxes divided by corporate taxable income) is lower than 35 percent because of tax credits and the lower tax rates that apply to the first $10 million of income. This option would increase all corporate income tax rates by 1 percentage point. For example, the corporate income tax rate would increase to 36 percent for taxable income above $10 million.

Option 64

Repeal the "LIFO" and "Lower of Cost or Market" Inventory Accounting Methods

(Billions of dollars)	2015	2016	2017	2018	2019	2020	2021	2022	2023	2024	2015-2019	2015-2024
Change in Revenues	13	26	26	26	14	2	2	2	2	2	104	115

Source: Staff of the Joint Committee on Taxation.

Note: This option would take effect in January 2015. Estimates are relative to CBO's April 2014 baseline projections.

To compute its taxable income, a business must first deduct from its receipts the cost of purchasing or producing the goods it sold during the year. Determining those costs requires that the business identify and attach a value to its inventory. The tax code allows firms to choose from among several approaches for identifying and determining the value of the goods included in their inventory. For itemizing and valuing goods in stock, firms can use the "specific identification" method which requires a very detailed physical accounting of items in inventory. An alternative approach—"last in, first out" (LIFO)—also allows firms to value their inventory at cost but permits them to assume that the last goods added to inventory were the first ones sold. Yet another alternative approach—"first in, first out" (FIFO)—is based on the assumption that the first goods sold from a business's inventory reflect the cost of the goods that have been in that inventory the longest. Firms that use the FIFO approach have two alternative methods for assessing the value of goods—the "lower of cost or market" (LCM) method allows them to assess inventory on the basis of its market value and use that valuation if it is lower than the cost. In addition, businesses that use the FIFO approach can qualify for the "subnormal-goods" method of inventory valuation if their goods cannot be sold at market prices because they are damaged or flawed.

This option would eliminate the LIFO method of identifying inventory, as well as the LCM and subnormal-goods methods of inventory valuation. Businesses would be required to use the specific-identification or FIFO methods to account for goods in their inventory and to set the value of that inventory on the basis of cost.

Option 65

Repeal Certain Tax Preferences for Extractive Industries

(Billions of dollars)	2015	2016	2017	2018	2019	2020	2021	2022	2023	2024	2015-2019	2015-2024
Change in Revenues												
Repeal the expensing of exploration and development costs	1.7	2.5	2.3	2.1	1.9	1.6	1.1	0.7	0.6	0.9	10.5	15.1
Disallow the use of the percentage depletion allowance	1.3	2.0	2.0	2.1	2.2	2.2	2.3	2.4	2.4	2.4	9.6	21.3

Source: Staff of the Joint Committee on Taxation.

Note: This option would take effect in January 2015. Estimates are relative to CBO's April 2014 baseline projections.

When calculating their taxable income, firms in most industrial sectors in the United States are generally allowed to deduct a portion of the investment costs they incurred that year and in previous years. The portion of those costs that is deductible depends on prescribed rates of depreciation or, for certain natural resources, depletion. Costs are deducted over a number of years to reflect an asset's rate of depreciation or depletion.

In contrast, the U.S. tax code treats extractive industries that produce oil, natural gas, coal, and hard minerals more favorably. Two tax preferences in particular give extractive industries an advantage over other industries:

■ One preference allows producers of oil, gas, coal, and minerals to "expense" some of the costs associated with exploration and development. Expensing allows companies to fully deduct such costs as they are incurred rather than waiting for those activities to generate income.

■ A second preference allows extractive industries to use a "percentage depletion allowance." Through that allowance, certain extractive companies can deduct from their taxable income between 5 percent and 22 percent of the dollar value of material extracted during the year, depending on the type of resource and up to certain limits. For each property they own, firms take a deduction for the greater of the percentage depletion allowance or the amount prescribed by the cost depletion system, which allows for recovery of investment costs as income is earned from those investments.

This option includes two different approaches to limiting tax preferences for extractive industries. The first approach would replace the expensing of exploration and development costs for oil, gas, coal, and hard minerals with the rules for deducting costs that apply in other industries. The second approach would eliminate the percentage depletion allowance.

Option 66

Extend the Period for Depreciating the Cost of Certain Investments

(Billions of dollars)	2015	2016	2017	2018	2019	2020	2021	2022	2023	2024	2015-2019	2015-2024
Change in Revenues	7	21	31	34	35	35	29	21	16	13	128	241

Source: Staff of the Joint Committee on Taxation.

Note: This option would take effect in January 2015. Estimates are relative to CBO's April 2014 baseline projections.

When calculating their taxable income, companies can deduct the expenses they incurred when producing tangible goods or providing services for sale, including depreciation—the drop in the value of a productive asset over time. The tax code sets the number of years, or service life, over which the value of different types of investments can be deducted from taxable income. Equipment and structures are the two main types of tangible capital for which businesses take depreciation deductions, and the effective tax rates on the income generated by those types of capital are currently quite different. (Effective tax rates measure the impact of statutory tax rates and other features of the tax code in the form of a single tax rate that

applies over the life of an investment.) The effective tax rates among equipment also differ depending on the lifespan of each piece of equipment.

This option would extend the lifetime of equipment and certain structures placed into service after December 31, 2014, for purposes of tax depreciation, with an aim toward equalizing the effective tax rates on income generated by different types of investment. Specifically, where the tax code currently stipulates a lifetime of 3, 5, 7, 10, 15, or 20 years for a given type of equipment, this option would increase those lifespans to 4, 7, 9, 13, 20, or 25 years, respectively.

Option 67

Repeal the Deduction for Domestic Production Activities

(Billions of dollars)	2015	2016	2017	2018	2019	2020	2021	2022	2023	2024	2015-2019	2015-2024
Change in Revenues	8	19	19	19	20	20	21	21	22	22	85	190

Source: Staff of the Joint Committee on Taxation.

Note: This option would take effect in January 2015. Estimates are relative to CBO's April 2014 baseline projections.

Businesses are allowed to deduct from their taxable income a percentage of what they earn from qualified domestic production activities. Various activities qualify for the deduction:

- Lease, rental, sale, exchange, or other disposition of tangible personal property, computer software, or sound recordings, if they are manufactured, produced, grown, or extracted in whole or significant part in the United States;

- Production of films (other than those that are sexually explicit);

- Production of electricity, natural gas, or potable water;

- Construction or renovation of real property; and

- Performance of engineering or architectural services.

The list of qualified activities specifically excludes the sale of food or beverages prepared at retail establishments; the transmission or distribution of electricity, natural gas, or potable water; and many activities that would otherwise qualify except that the proceeds come from sales to a related business.

This option would repeal the deduction for domestic production activities.

Option 68

Repeal the Low-Income Housing Tax Credit

(Billions of dollars)	2015	2016	2017	2018	2019	2020	2021	2022	2023	2024	2015-2019	2015-2024
Change in Revenues	0.4	0.5	1.2	2.1	3.1	4.1	5.2	6.2	7.4	8.4	7.3	38.6

Source: Staff of the Joint Committee on Taxation.

Note: This option would take effect in January 2015. Estimates are relative to CBO's April 2014 baseline projections.

Real estate developers who provide rental housing for low-income households may qualify for the low-income housing tax credit, which is designed to encourage investment in affordable housing. The credit covers a portion of the costs incurred for the construction of new housing units, the substantial rehabilitation of existing units, and the purchase of land on which new housing units will be built.

This option would repeal the low-income housing tax credit starting in calendar year 2015, although projects granted credits before that year could continue to claim them until their eligibility expired.

Option 69

Modify the Rules for the Sourcing of Income From Exports

(Billions of dollars)	2015	2016	2017	2018	2019	2020	2021	2022	2023	2024	2015-2019	2015-2024
Change in Revenues	0.2	0.4	0.5	0.5	0.4	0.4	0.4	0.4	0.4	0.4	2.0	3.9

Source: Staff of the Joint Committee on Taxation.

Note: This option would take effect in January 2015. Estimates are relative to CBO's April 2014 baseline projections.

To prevent the income that U.S. corporations earn abroad from being subject to both foreign and U.S. taxation, the federal government provides a credit for taxes paid to foreign governments. Under the rules governing that tax credit, it cannot exceed the amount of U.S. tax those businesses otherwise would have owed on their foreign income.

To calculate the limit on foreign taxes, a firm's income must be allocated between foreign and domestic sources. For the purposes of determining the foreign tax credit, the U.S. tax code distinguishes between two categories of income derived from the sale of goods: Income resulting from the sale of goods that a U.S. firm buys from another business and then resells abroad; and income resulting from the sale of goods that a U.S. firm manufactures and then sells directly to buyers in other countries. Income in the first category is governed by the U.S. tax code's "title passage rule," which specifies that such earnings be "sourced" in the country where the sale occurs. However, for the second category of income, a special rule applies: When the goods are produced in the United States and then sold by that firm to foreign buyers, half of the resulting income is sourced in the United States; the rest of the income is subject to the title passage rule and allocated to the country where the sale took place.

Under this option, the title passage rule would no longer apply to income from the sale of goods manufactured in the United States and then sold abroad. Instead, all income from such transactions would be sourced to the United States.

Option 70

Increase Excise Taxes on Motor Fuels by 35 Cents and Index for Inflation

(Billions of dollars)	2015	2016	2017	2018	2019	2020	2021	2022	2023	2024	2015- 2019	2015- 2024
Change in Revenues	32	45	46	47	48	49	50	50	51	52	217	469

Source: Staff of the Joint Committee on Taxation.

Note: This option would take effect in January 2015. Estimates are relative to CBO's April 2014 baseline projections. Because excise taxes reduce producers' and consumers' income, higher excise taxes would lead to reductions in revenues from income and payroll taxes. The estimates shown here reflect those reductions.

Revenues from federal excise taxes on motor fuels are credited to the Highway Trust Fund to pay for highway construction and maintenance as well as for investment in mass transit. This option would increase federal excise taxes on gasoline and diesel fuel by 35 cents per gallon, to 53.4 cents per gallon of gasoline and 59.4 cents per gallon of diesel fuel. In future years, those values would be adjusted to reflect changes in the price index for gross domestic product between calendar year 2015 and the most recent year for which data for that price index were available.

Option 71

Increase All Taxes on Alcoholic Beverages to $16 per Proof Gallon

(Billions of dollars)	2015	2016	2017	2018	2019	2020	2021	2022	2023	2024	2015- 2019	2015- 2024
Change in Revenues	4.8	6.4	6.5	6.6	6.7	6.8	6.9	7.0	7.1	7.2	31.0	65.9

Source: Staff of the Joint Committee on Taxation.

Note: This option would take effect in January 2015. Estimates are relative to CBO's April 2014 baseline projections. Because excise taxes reduce producers' and consumers' income, higher excise taxes would lead to reductions in revenues from income and payroll taxes. The estimates shown here reflect those reductions.

The federal government collects revenue from excise taxes on distilled spirits, beer, and wine. The different alcoholic beverages are taxed at different rates. This option would standardize the base on which the federal excise tax is applied by using the proof gallon as the measure with the tax levied at $16 per proof gallon for all alcoholic beverages. A tax of $16 per proof gallon would equal about 25 cents per ounce of alcohol. Under this option, the federal excise tax on a 750-milliliter bottle (commonly referred to as a fifth) of distilled spirits would rise from about $2.14 to $2.54. The tax on a six-pack of beer would jump from about 33 cents to 81 cents, and the tax on a 750-milliliter bottle of wine would increase by a similar amount, from about 21 cents to 70 cents.

Option 72

Limit Medical Malpractice Torts

(Billions of dollars)	2015	2016	2017	2018	2019	2020	2021	2022	2023	2024	2015-2019	2015-2024
Change in Mandatory Outlays[a]	-0.1	-1.3	-3.7	-5.7	-7.0	-7.5	-8.0	-8.8	-9.1	-9.3	-17.7	-60.4
Change in Revenues[b]	*	0.1	0.4	0.7	0.9	1.0	1.0	1.1	1.2	1.2	2.1	7.6
Change in Discretionary Outlays	*	*	-0.1	-0.2	-0.2	-0.2	-0.3	-0.3	-0.3	-0.3	-0.6	-2.0

Sources: Congressional Budget Office; staff of the Joint Committee on Taxation.

Notes: This option would take effect in January 2015. Estimates are relative to CBO's August 2014 baseline projections.

　　* = between -$50 million and $50 million.

a.　Estimates include potential savings by the Postal Service, whose spending is classified as off-budget.

b.　Estimates include the effects on Social Security payroll tax receipts, which are classified as off-budget.

Individuals may pursue civil claims against physicians, hospitals, and other health care providers for alleged torts, which, in the medical field, primarily include breaches of duty that result in personal injury. This option would limit medical malpractice torts nationwide in several ways:

■ Capping awards for noneconomic damages (also known as pain and suffering) at $250,000;

■ Capping awards for punitive damages at $500,000 or at two times the value of awards for economic damages (such as for lost income and medical costs), whichever is greater;

■ Shortening the statute of limitations to one year from the date of discovery of an injury for adults and to three years for children;

■ Establishing a fair-share rule (in which a defendant in a lawsuit is liable only for the percentage of a final award that is equal to his or her share of responsibility for the injury) to replace the current rule of joint-and-several liability (in which all of the defendants are individually responsible for the entire amount of the award);

■ Allowing evidence of income from collateral sources (such as life insurance payouts and health insurance) to be introduced at trial; and

■ Imposing sliding-scale limits on the contingency fees that lawyers can charge.

For this option, CBO expects that changes enacted in January 2015 would take four years to have their full impact, as providers gradually modified their practice patterns.

Option 73

Introduce Minimum Out-of-Pocket Requirements Under TRICARE for Life

(Billions of dollars)	2015	2016	2017	2018	2019	2020	2021	2022	2023	2024	2015-2019	2015-2024
Change in Mandatory Outlays												
MERHCF	0	0	-1.2	-2.0	-2.2	-2.4	-2.5	-2.7	-2.9	-3.0	-5.4	-18.9
Medicare	0	0	-0.4	-0.9	-1.1	-1.2	-1.2	-1.3	-1.4	-1.5	-2.4	-9.0
Total	0	0	-1.6	-2.9	-3.3	-3.5	-3.8	-4.0	-4.3	-4.5	-7.8	-27.9

Notes: This option would take effect in January 2017. Estimates are relative to CBO's August 2014 baseline projections.

MERHCF = Department of Defense Medicare-Eligible Retiree Health Care Fund.

TRICARE for Life (TFL) is a supplement to Medicare for military retirees and their family members who are eligible for Medicare. The program pays nearly all medical costs not covered by Medicare and requires few out-of-pocket fees. This option would introduce minimum out-of-pocket requirements for TFL beneficiaries. For calendar year 2017, TFL would not cover any of the first $650 of an enrollee's cost-sharing payments under Medicare and would cover only 50 percent of the next $5,850 in such payments. Those dollar limits would be indexed to growth in average Medicare costs (excluding Part D drug benefits) for later years. This option also would require TFL beneficiaries seeking care from military treatment facilities to make payments that would be roughly comparable to the charges they would face at civilian facilities.

Option 74

Change the Cost-Sharing Rules for Medicare and Restrict Medigap Insurance

(Billions of dollars)	2015	2016	2017	2018	2019	2020	2021	2022	2023	2024	2015-2019	2015-2024
Change in Mandatory Outlays												
Establish uniform cost sharing for Medicare	0	0	-4	-6	-6	-7	-7	-7	-8	-9	-16	-54
Restrict medigap plans	0	0	-4	-6	-6	-7	-7	-7	-8	-8	-16	-53
Both of the above policies[a]	0	0	-9	-12	-13	-14	-15	-16	-17	-18	-33	-111

Note: This option would take effect in January 2017. Estimates are relative to CBO's April 2014 baseline projections.

a.   If both policies were enacted together, the total effects would be greater than the sum of the effects for each policy because of interactions between the approaches.

CBO examined three alternative ways to reduce federal spending on Medicare by modifying the cost sharing that fee-for-service enrollees face. The alternatives would apply to all enrollees. The budgetary effects of changing Medicare's cost-sharing rules depend significantly on the specific parameters chosen.

The first alternative would replace Medicare's current mix of cost-sharing requirements. A single annual deductible of $650 would cover all services a patient obtained under Medicare's Part A (Hospital Insurance) and Part B (Medical Insurance), a uniform coinsurance rate of 20 percent would apply for amounts above the deductible (including coverage for inpatient expenses), and there would be an annual cap of $6,500 on each enrollee's total cost sharing. (Prescription drug coverage under Part D would not be changed.) The changes would take effect on January 1, 2017, and the dollar amounts of the various thresholds would be indexed to increase in later years at the same rate as average fee-for-service Medicare costs per enrollee.

The second alternative would leave Medicare's cost-sharing rules unchanged and would not affect employment-based supplemental coverage but would restrict current and future medigap policies—individual insurance policies providing supplemental coverage of most or all of Medicare's cost-sharing requirements.

Specifically, it would bar those policies from paying any of the first $650 of an enrollee's cost-sharing obligations and would limit their coverage to 50 percent of the next $5,850 of an enrollee's cost sharing. Medigap policies would cover all further cost sharing, so policyholders would not pay more than $3,575 in cost sharing in 2017. The changes would take effect on January 1, 2017, and the dollar amounts of the various thresholds would be indexed as specified in the first alternative.

The third alternative combines the changes from the first two. Thus, in calendar year 2017, all medigap plans would be prohibited from covering any of the new $650 combined deductible for Part A and Part B services, and the annual cap on an enrollee's out-of-pocket obligations, including payments by supplemental plans on an enrollee's behalf, would be limited to $6,500. For spending that occurred after meeting the deductible but before reaching the cap, medigap policyholders would face a uniform coinsurance rate of 10 percent for all services, whereas Medicare enrollees without supplemental coverage would face a uniform coinsurance rate of 20 percent for all services. Those provisions would limit the out-of-pocket spending of medigap enrollees (excluding medigap premiums) to $3,575 and the out-of-pocket spending of Medicare enrollees without supplemental coverage to $6,500.

Option 75

Increase Premiums for Parts B and D of Medicare

(Billions of dollars)	2015	2016	2017	2018	2019	2020	2021	2022	2023	2024	2015-2019	2015-2024
Change in Mandatory Outlays												
Increase basic premiums	0	-5	-12	-19	-29	-40	-43	-48	-51	-53	-65	-299
Freeze income thresholds for income-related premiums	0	0	0	0	0	-3	-4	-5	-6	-8	0	-25
Both of the above policies[a]	0	-5	-12	-19	-29	-41	-45	-51	-54	-57	-65	-314

Note: The first and third alternatives would take effect in January 2016; the second alternative would take effect in January 2020. Estimates are relative to CBO's August 2014 baseline projections.

a.   If both policies were enacted together, the total effects would be less than the sum of the effects for each policy because of interactions between the approaches.

All enrollees in Part B of Medicare (which covers physicians' and other outpatient services) or Part D (which covers prescription drugs) are charged basic premiums for that coverage. Enrollees in Parts B and D who have relatively high income pay a higher premium known as the income-related premium (IRP). The amount of the IRP depends on an enrollee's modified adjusted gross income, or MAGI (the total of adjusted gross income and tax-exempt interest). The MAGI thresholds established for income-related premiums create four income brackets and premiums that correspond to them. For 2015 through 2019, the income thresholds at which IRPs begin for both Parts B and D are $85,000 for single beneficiaries and $170,000 for married couples who file joint tax returns. Those income thresholds will be increased in 2020 and subsequent years to the levels they would have reached had they been indexed for inflation since 2007.

This option would raise the premiums for Parts B and D of Medicare in various ways (years mentioned in this option are calendar years):

■ The first alternative would increase the basic premiums from 25 percent of Part B costs per enrollee and 25.5 percent of Part D costs per enrollee to 35 percent of both programs' costs; that increase would occur gradually over a five-year period beginning in 2016. For Part B, the percentage of costs per enrollee covered by the basic premium would rise by 2 percentage points a year through 2020 and then remain at 35 percent. For Part D, that percentage would increase by 1.5 percentage points in the first year and 2 percentage points a year from 2017 through 2020 and then remain at 35 percent.

■ The second alternative would freeze through 2024 all of the income thresholds for income-related premiums.

■ The third alternative would combine the changes in the first two: increasing basic premiums for Parts B and D to 35 percent of costs per enrollee and freezing the income thresholds for income-related premiums.

Option 76

Require Manufacturers to Pay a Minimum Rebate on Drugs Covered Under Part D of Medicare for Low-Income Beneficiaries

(Billions of dollars)	2015	2016	2017	2018	2019	2020	2021	2022	2023	2024	2015-2019	2015-2024
Change in Mandatory Outlays	0	*	-5	-12	-14	-14	-14	-13	-14	-17	-31	-103

Notes: This option would take effect in January 2017. Estimates are relative to CBO's August 2014 baseline projections.

* = between zero and $500 million.

Before the establishment of Part D in 2006, Medicare beneficiaries who were also eligible for full benefits from Medicaid—known as "dual-eligible beneficiaries"—received drug coverage through Medicaid. That program requires drug manufacturers to pay state and federal governments a significant rebate on their sales to Medicaid enrollees. The rebate amount is currently 23.1 percent of the price that manufacturers receive for sales to retail pharmacies (known as the average manufacturer price). Additional rebates are required if a drug's price rises faster than overall inflation.

When Part D of Medicare was established, dual-eligible beneficiaries were enrolled automatically in a low-income-subsidy (LIS) program in Part D, which typically covers the premiums and most of the cost sharing required under the basic Part D benefit. Currently, the rebates for drugs used by LIS enrollees are established in the same way as those for drugs used by other Part D enrollees: through negotiations between private Part D plans and drug makers.

This option would require manufacturers of brand-name drugs to pay the federal government a rebate on drugs purchased by enrollees in the Part D LIS program, starting in calendar year 2017. As with the current rebate system for Medicaid, manufacturers would have to pay a total rebate of at least 23.1 percent of a drug's average manufacturer price, plus an additional rebate for price increases that exceeded the rate of inflation since the drug's introduction. If a drug manufacturer already provides discounts or rebates to Part D plans that apply equally to all Part D enrollees, any difference between those discounts or rebates and the total rebate amount that the manufacturer would owe under this option would be paid to the federal government. Manufacturers would be required to participate in this rebate program in order to have their drugs covered by Parts B and D of Medicare, by Medicaid, and by the Veterans Health Administration.

Option 77

Modify TRICARE Enrollment Fees and Cost Sharing for Working-Age Military Retirees

(Billions of dollars)	2015	2016	2017	2018	2019	2020	2021	2022	2023	2024	2015-2019	2015-2024
				Modify TRICARE Enrollment Fees, Deductibles, and Copayments								
Change in Mandatory Outlays	0	*	*	*	*	*	*	*	*	*	-0.1	-0.3
Change in Revenues[a]	0	*	-0.1	-0.1	-0.2	-0.2	-0.2	-0.3	-0.3	-0.3	-0.4	-1.7
Change in Discretionary Spending												
Budget authority	0	-1.0	-1.4	-2.0	-2.1	-2.3	-2.5	-2.7	-3.0	-3.2	-6.5	-20.3
Outlays	0	-0.8	-1.3	-1.8	-2.0	-2.2	-2.4	-2.6	-2.8	-3.1	-5.9	-19.0
				Make Retirees Ineligible for TRICARE Prime								
Change in Mandatory Outlays	0	*	0.1	0.1	0.1	0.1	0.2	0.2	0.2	0.2	0.3	1.2
Change in Revenues[a]	0	-0.2	-0.6	-1.1	-1.3	-1.5	-1.6	-1.7	-1.8	-1.9	-3.2	-11.7
Change in Discretionary Spending												
Budget authority	0	-3.7	-5.6	-7.9	-8.4	-8.9	-9.5	-10.1	-10.7	-11.4	-25.6	-76.1
Outlays	0	-2.9	-5.1	-7.3	-8.1	-8.8	-9.3	-9.9	-10.5	-11.2	-23.4	-73.2

Sources: Congressional Budget Office; staff of the Joint Committee on Taxation.

Notes: This option would take effect in October 2015. Estimates are relative to CBO's August 2014 baseline projections.

   * = between -$50 million and $50 million.

a.   Negative numbers denote a reduction in revenues.

This option comprises two alternatives that would reduce future growth in military health care spending by requiring working-age military retirees and their families to pay more for TRICARE. Such individuals are currently eligible to enroll in TRICARE Prime, a plan that operates like a health maintenance organization. Military retirees who do not enroll in TRICARE Prime may receive benefits under TRICARE Standard (a traditional fee-for-service plan) or Extra (a preferred provider network).

The first alternative would raise the enrollment fees, deductibles, and copayments for working-age military retirees who want to use TRICARE. The second alternative would make working-age military retirees and their families ineligible for TRICARE Prime, which is the most costly of the three programs for the Department of Defense. Those people could instead enroll in TRICARE Standard or Extra, although they would pay a monthly premium that would be set at 28 percent of the average cost of providing Standard or Extra benefits for that group.

Option 78

Reduce or Constrain Funding for the National Institutes of Health

(Billions of dollars)	2015	2016	2017	2018	2019	2020	2021	2022	2023	2024	2015-2019	2015-2024
					Restrict the Growth of Funding to 1 Percent a Year							
Change in Discretionary Spending												
Budget authority	0	-0.1	-0.4	-0.8	-1.2	-1.6	-2.0	-2.4	-2.8	-3.3	-2.6	-14.7
Outlays	0	*	-0.2	-0.5	-0.8	-1.2	-1.6	-2.0	-2.4	-2.8	-1.5	-11.5
					Reduce 2016 Funding and Allow Growth at the Rate of Inflation							
Change in Discretionary Spending												
Budget authority	0	-4.1	-4.1	-4.2	-4.3	-4.4	-4.5	-4.6	-4.7	-4.8	-16.7	-39.7
Outlays	0	-1.1	-3.3	-3.9	-4.2	-4.3	-4.4	-4.5	-4.6	-4.7	-12.4	-34.7

Notes: This option would take effect in October 2015. Estimates are relative to CBO's August 2014 baseline projections.

    * = between -$50 million and zero.

In 2013, the National Institutes of Health (NIH) accounted for nearly half of all nondefense discretionary spending for research and development. (All years mentioned in this option are fiscal years.) This option consists of two alternatives that would reduce NIH's appropriations relative to the amounts in the baseline budget projections of the Congressional Budget Office.

One alternative would restrict the rate of growth in appropriations to 1 percent per year. The other alternative would reduce NIH's 2016 appropriation by about 13 percent to the amount provided in 2003, the last year in which NIH had a large increase in its appropriation; after 2016, funding would grow at the rate of inflation incorporated in CBO's baseline projections.

Option 79

Increase the Excise Tax on Cigarettes by 50 Cents per Pack

(Billions of dollars)	2015	2016	2017	2018	2019	2020	2021	2022	2023	2024	2015-2019	2015-2024
Change in Outlays	*	*	*	-0.1	-0.1	-0.1	-0.1	-0.1	-0.1	-0.1	-0.2	-0.6
Change in Revenues[a]	3.1	3.8	3.6	3.6	3.5	3.5	3.5	3.4	3.4	3.3	17.6	34.7
Net Effect on the Deficit	-3.1	-3.8	-3.6	-3.6	-3.6	-3.6	-3.6	-3.5	-3.5	-3.4	-17.7	-35.3

Sources: Staff of the Joint Committee on Taxation; Congressional Budget Office.

Notes: This option would take effect in January 2015. Estimates are relative to CBO's August 2014 baseline projections. Because excise taxes reduce producers' and consumers' income, higher excise taxes would lead to reductions in revenues from income and payroll taxes. The estimates shown here reflect those reductions.

    * = between -$50 million and zero.

a. Positive numbers denote an increase in revenues.

Both the federal government and state governments tax tobacco products. Currently, the federal excise tax on cigarettes is $1.01 per pack. This option would raise the federal excise tax on cigarettes by 50 cents per pack beginning in calendar year 2015. That rate increase

would also apply to small cigars, which are generally viewed as a close substitute for cigarettes and are currently taxed by the federal government at the same rate as cigarettes.

Appendix:
Some Options for Deficit Reduction
Not Included in This Report

This appendix lists options that the Congressional Budget Office (CBO) has analyzed previously but for which no budgetary estimates are presented. Those options are drawn from two sources. Some were analyzed in *Options for Reducing the Deficit: 2014 to 2023* (November 2013) but would take considerable time to reanalyze; in order to make this document available prior to the beginning of the 114th Congress in January 2015, those options are listed here without updated estimates. Others, taken from various CBO reports, were brought forward from the similar listing in Appendix A of the November 2013 report.

Certain options from those two sources are not included in this appendix for one of two reasons. Some were omitted because they have been superseded by subsequent legislation or administrative action. Others were excluded because earlier budgetary estimates are probably no longer useful because of changes arising from legislation or administrative action, economic developments, or other aspects of CBO's analysis.

Table A-1.

Selected Deficit Reduction Options That Appeared in Previous CBO Reports

	Original Publication[a] (Option Number)
Mandatory Spending Options (Other than those for health-related programs)	
Budget Function 270: Energy	
Transfer the Tennessee Valley Authority's Electric Utility Functions and Associated Assets and Liabilities	G (2)
Reduce the Size of the Strategic Petroleum Reserve	G (3)
Budget Function 300: Natural Resources and Environment	
Reassign Reimbursable Costs for the Pick-Sloan Missouri Basin Program to the Beneficiaries It Serves	I (300-8)
Budget Function 350: Agriculture	
Eliminate the Foreign Market Development Program	I (350-4)
Reduce Funding for the Market Access Program	I (350-5)
Limit the Repayment Period for Export Credit Guarantees	I (350-6)
Budget Function 370: Commerce and Housing Credit	
Permanently Extend the Federal Communications Commission's Authority to Auction Licenses for Use of the Radio Spectrum	I (370-3)
Budget Function 600: Income Security	
Decrease the Maximum Benefit for the Supplemental Nutrition Assistance Program to 97 Percent of the Cost of the Thrifty Food Plan	F
Eliminate the Exclusion for Unearned Income Under the Supplemental Security Income Program	I (600-7)
Create a Sliding Scale for Children's Supplemental Security Income Benefits Based on the Number of Recipients in a Family	I (600-8)
Remove the Ceiling on the Collection of Overpayments From the Supplemental Security Income Program	I (600-9)
Budget Function 650: Social Security	
Reduce DI Benefits for People Age 53 and Older	E
Increase the Age at Which Disability Requirements Become Less Restrictive	E
Raise the Earliest Eligibility Age for Social Security	G (29)
Apply the Social Security Benefit Formula to Individual Years of Earnings	G (32)
Extend the Waiting Period for DI Benefits From 5 Months to 12 Months	E
Reduce the Top Two PIA Factors By Roughly One-Third	H (13)
Reduce COLAs By 0.5 Percentage Points	H (29)
Reduce the Spousal Benefit in Social Security From 50 Percent to 33 Percent	I (650-5)
Eliminate the Social Security Lump-Sum Death Benefit	I (650-6)
Require Children Under Age 18 to Attend School Full Time as a Condition of Eligibility for Social Security Benefits	I (650-7)
Eliminate Social Security Benefits for Children of Early Retirees	I (650-8)
Require State and Local Pension Plans to Share Data With the Social Security Administration	I (650-9)
Budget Function 700: Veterans Benefits and Services	
Reduce Veterans' Disability Compensation to Account for Social Security DI Payments	I (700-1)
Budget Function 800: General Government	
Require the IRS to Deposit Fees for Its Services in the Treasury as Miscellaneous Receipts	I (800-2)

Continued

Table A-1.   Continued

Selected Deficit Reduction Options That Appeared in Previous CBO Reports

	Original Publication[a] (Option Number)
Discretionary Spending Options[b] (Other than those for health-related programs)	
Budget Function 050: National Defense	
Reduce the Size of the Military to Satisfy Caps Under the Budget Control Act	A (Discretionary-1)
Consolidate the Department of Defense's Retail Activities and Provide a Grocery Allowance to Service Members	G (6)
Consolidate and Encourage Efficiencies in Military Exchanges	I (050-18)
Substitute Dependent Education Allowances for Domestic On-Base Schools	I (050-20)
Ease Restrictions on Contracting for Depot Maintenance	I (050-22)
Budget Function 250: General Science, Space, and Technology	
Eliminate National Science Foundation Spending on Elementary and Secondary Education	I (250-1)
Reduce Funding for Research and Development Programs in the Science and Technology Directorate of the Department of Homeland Security	I (250-3)
Budget Function 300: Natural Resources and Environment	
Eliminate the Energy Star Program	I (300-10)
Eliminate the Environmental Protection Agency's Science to Achieve Results Grant Program	I (300-11)
Eliminate the National Park Service's Local Funding for Heritage Area Grants and Statutory Aid	I (300-15)
Budget Function 370: Commerce and Housing Credit	
Eliminate the Hollings Manufacturing Extension Partnership and the Baldrige National Quality Program	I (370-2)
Impose Fees on the Small Business Administration's Secondary Market Guarantees	I (370-4)
Budget Function 400: Transportation	
Increase Fees for Aviation Security	A (Discretionary-17)
Eliminate the Essential Air Service Program	I (400-5)
Budget Function 450: Community and Regional Development	
Eliminate NeighborWorks America	I (450-2)
Eliminate the Community Development Financial Institutions Fund	I (450-3)
Create State Revolving Funds to Finance Rural Water and Waste Disposal	I (450-4)
Eliminate Regional Development Agencies	I (450-5)
Restrict First-Responder Grants to High-Risk Communities	I (450-6)
Budget Function 500: Education, Training, Employment, and Social Services	
Restrict Pell Grants to Students Who Meet More Stringent Academic Eligibility Requirements	B
Restrict Pell Grants to Students Who Meet Academic Progress Requirements	B
Eliminate Administrative Fees Paid to Schools in the Campus-Based Student Aid and Pell Grant Programs	I (500-8)
Budget Function 600: Income Security	
Reduce Rent Subsidies for Certain One-Person Households	I (600-5)
Budget Function 750: Administration of Justice	
Eliminate the Legal Services Corporation	I (750-2)
Budget Function 800: General Government	
Eliminate General Fiscal Assistance to the District of Columbia	I (800-1)
Eliminate the National Youth Anti-Drug Media Campaign	I (800-4)

Continued

Table A-1. Continued

Selected Deficit Reduction Options That Appeared in Previous CBO Reports

	Original Publication[a] (Option Number)
Revenue Options (Other than those related to health)	
Individual Income Tax Base	
Include Employer-Paid Premiums for Income Replacement Insurance in Employees' Taxable Income	A (Revenues-9)
Include Investment Income From Life Insurance and Annuities in Taxable Income	A (Revenues-10)
Tax Carried Interest as Ordinary Income	A (Revenues-11)
Gradually Eliminate the Mortgage Interest Deduction	G (4)
Replace the Tax Exclusion for Interest Income on State and Local Bonds With a Direct Subsidy for the Issuer	G (13)
Limit Deductions for Charitable Gifts of Appreciated Assets to the Gifts' Tax Basis	I (11)
Eliminate Tax Subsidies for Child and Dependent Care	I (13)
Eliminate the Additional Standard Deduction for Elderly and Blind Taxpayers	I (14)
Eliminate the Tax Exclusion for Employment-Based Life Insurance	I (16)
End the Preferential Treatment of Dividends Paid on Stock Held in Employee Stock Ownership Plans	I (22)
Individual Income Tax Credits	
Eliminate the EITC for People Who Do Not Live With Children	I (23)
Include Social Security Benefits in Calculating the Phase-Out of the EITC	I (24)
Corporate Income Tax Rates	
Set the Corporate Income Tax Rate at 35 Percent for All Corporations	G (19)
Taxation of Income From Businesses and Other Entities	
Treat Large Pass-Through Entities as C Corporations	D
Eliminate the Subchapter S Option and Tax Limited Liability Companies as C Corporations	D
Tax Large Credit Unions in the Same Way as Other Thrift Institutions	I (32)
Tax the Income Earned By Public Electric Utilities	I (34)
Cap Nonprofit Organizations' Outstanding Stock of Tax-Exempt Bonds	I (39)
Tax the Federal Home Loan Banks Under the Corporate Income Tax	I (42)
Tax Qualified Sponsorship Payments to Postsecondary Sports Programs	I (43)
Taxation of Income From Worldwide Business Activity	
Determine Foreign Tax Credits on a Pooling Basis	A (Revenues-30)
Eliminate Check-the-Box Rules	C
Defer Interest Deductions Related to Deferred Income	C
Tax the Worldwide Income of U.S. Corporations as it Is Earned	C
Taxation of Payroll Income	
Expand Social Security Coverage to Include Newly Hired State and Local Government Employees	A (Revenues-19)
Tax All Pass-Through Business Owners Under SECA and Impose a Material Participation Standard	A (Revenues-21)
Raise the DI Tax Rate by 0.4 Percentage Points	E
Require Self-Employed People and Employees to Pay the Same Amounts in Payroll Taxes	I (46)
Other Taxes and Fees	
Impose a Tax on Financial Transactions	A (Revenues-33)
Impose a Fee on Large Financial Institutions	A (Revenues-34)
Impose a Tax on Emissions of Greenhouse Gases	A (Revenues-35)
Impose a 5 Percent Value-Added Tax	G (27)
Reinstate the Superfund Taxes	G (34)
Impose a Tax on Emissions of Sulfur Dioxide	I (55)
Impose a Tax on Emissions of Nitrogen Oxides	I (56)
Finance the Food Safety and Inspection Service Solely Through Fees	I (65)

Continued

Selected Deficit Reduction Options That Appeared in Previous CBO Reports

	Original Publication[a] (Option Number)
Health Options	
Budget Function 550: Health	
Impose Caps on Federal Spending for Medicaid	A (Health-1)
Add a "Public Plan" to the Health Insurance Exchanges	A (Health-2)
Eliminate Exchange Subsidies for People With Income Over 300 Percent of the Federal Poverty Guidelines	A (Health-3)
Adopt a Voucher Plan and Slow the Growth of Federal Contributions for the Federal Employees Health Benefits Program	G (Mandatory-14)
Budget Function 570: Medicare	
Convert Medicare to a Premium Support System	A (Health-6)
Raise the Age of Eligibility for Medicare to 67	A (Health-8)
Bundle Medicare's Payments to Health Care Providers	A (Health-10)
Consolidate and Reduce Federal Payments for Graduate Medical Education Costs at Teaching Hospitals	G (Mandatory-17)
Reduce Medicare's Payment Rates Across the Board in High-Spending Areas	G (Mandatory-23)
Eliminate the Critical Access Hospital, Medicare-Dependent Hospital, and Sole Community Hospital Programs in Medicare	G (Mandatory-24)
Budget Function 700: Veterans Benefits and Services	
End Enrollment in VA Medical Care for Veterans in Priority Groups 7 and 8	A (Health-14)
Revenues	
Reduce Tax Preferences for Employment-Based Health Insurance	A (Health-15)
Repeal the Individual Health Insurance Mandate	G (Revenues-32)

Source: Congressional Budget Office.

Notes: The effects that CBO would estimate for these options now might differ from the amounts shown in the original publication for one or more of the following reasons: The baseline budget projections against which the option would be measured have changed, CBO has revised its estimating methodology, or the agency's judgments about the effects of the options span a different projection period.

Budget functions are the 20 general subject categories into which budget accounts are grouped so that all spending can be presented according to the national interests being addressed.

DI = Disability Insurance; PIA = primary insurance amount; COLA = cost-of-living adjustment; IRS = Internal Revenue Service; EITC = earned income tax credit; SECA = Self Employment Contributions Act; VA = Department of Veterans Affairs.

a.   The options listed appeared originally in the following CBO publications:

   A. *Options for Reducing the Deficit: 2014 to 2023* (November 2013), www.cbo.gov/budget-options/2013/44687

   B. *The Federal Pell Grant Program: Recent Growth and Policy Options* (September 2013), www.cbo.gov/publication/44448

   C. *Options for Taxing U.S. Multinational Corporations* (January 2013), www.cbo.gov/publication/43764

   D. *Taxing Businesses Through the Individual Income Tax* (December 2012), www.cbo.gov/publication/43750

   E. *Policy Options for the Social Security Disability Insurance Program* (July 2012), www.cbo.gov/publication/43421

   F. *The Supplemental Nutrition Assistance Program* (April 2012), www.cbo.gov/publication/43173

   G. *Reducing the Deficit: Spending and Revenue Options* (March 2011), www.cbo.gov/publication/22043

   H. *Social Security Policy Options* (July 2010), www.cbo.gov/publication/21547

   I. *Budget Options, Volume 2* (August 2009), www.cbo.gov/publication/41190

b.   To reduce deficits through changes in discretionary spending, lawmakers would need to reduce the statutory funding caps below the levels already established under current law or enact appropriations below those caps. The options listed here could be used to accomplish either of those objectives (although the savings shown for some of the defense options are measured relative to the Defense Department's plans rather than CBO's baseline projections). Alternatively, some of the options could be implemented to comply with the existing caps on discretionary funding rather than to reduce projected deficits.

About This Document

At the request of the House and Senate Committees on the Budget, the Congressional Budget Office (CBO) periodically issues a compendium of budget options to help inform federal lawmakers about the implications of possible policy choices. This volume presents 79 options for altering spending and revenues to reduce federal budget deficits.

The estimates presented in this document are updates of many of those presented in *Options for Reducing the Deficit: 2014 to 2023* (November 2013). But this volume omits some of the options included there because they have been superseded by subsequent legislation or administrative actions. Furthermore, to be available before the beginning of the 114th Congress, the document also omits some options included before because of the considerable time that would have been needed to reanalyze them.

The options included in this report originally came from a variety of sources, including legislative proposals, various Administrations' budget proposals, Congressional staff, other government entities, and private groups. The options are intended to reflect a range of possibilities rather than to provide a ranking of priorities or a comprehensive list. The inclusion or exclusion of a particular policy change does not represent an endorsement or rejection by CBO. In keeping with CBO's mandate to provide objective, impartial analysis, this report makes no recommendations.

This volume is the result of work by more than 100 people at CBO, whose names are listed on the following pages, as well as the staff of the Joint Committee on Taxation.

The report is available on CBO's website (www.cbo.gov/budget-options/2014/49638).

Douglas W. Elmendorf
Director

November 2014

The spending estimates that appear in this report were prepared by the staff of the Congressional Budget Office's Budget Analysis Division (supervised by Peter Fontaine, Theresa Gullo, Holly Harvey, Tom Bradley, Kim Cawley, Chad Chirico, Jeffrey Holland, Sarah Jennings, and Sam Papenfuss); Health, Retirement, and Long-Term Analysis Division (supervised by Linda Bilheimer, James Baumgardner, and Julie Topoleski); and Financial Analysis Division (supervised by Damien Moore). Most of the revenue estimates were prepared by the staff of the Joint Committee on Taxation, although some were done by CBO's Tax Analysis Division (supervised by David Weiner, Mark Booth, and Janet Holtzblatt) and Budget Analysis Division.

Mandatory Spending Options

Sheila Dacey of the Budget Analysis Division coordinated work on the options for mandatory spending, which was done by the following analysts:

Nabeel Alsalam	Andrea Noda
Elizabeth Bass	Sarah Puro
Sheila Dacey	David Rafferty
Molly Dahl	Lisa Ramirez-Branum
Elizabeth Cove Delisle	Daniel Ready
Justin Falk	Lara Robillard
Kathleen FitzGerald	Matthew Schmit
Katherine Fritzsche	Erica Socker
Heidi Golding	Emily Stern
Kathleen Gramp	Robert Stewart
Justin Humphrey	Andrew Stocking
Deborah Kalcevic	Aurora Swanson
Jeff LaFave	Natalie Tawil
James Langley	Julie Topoleski
William Ma	David Torregrosa
Amber Marcellino	Ellen Werble
Paul Masi	Dwayne Wright
Jamease Miles	Rebecca Yip
Carla Tighe Murray	

Discretionary Spending Options

Sunita D'Monte of the Budget Analysis Division coordinated work on the options for discretionary spending, which was done by the following analysts:

Adebayo Adedeji	Perry Beider
Nabeel Alsalam	Marin Burnett
Christina Hawley Anthony	Sheila Campbell
David Arthur	Megan Carroll

Discretionary Spending Options (Continued)

Chad Chirico	Jamease Miles
Julia Christensen	David Newman
Molly Dahl	Andrea Noda
Elizabeth Cove Delisle	Matthew Pickford
Sunita D'Monte	Sarah Puro
Justin Falk	Lisa Ramirez-Branum
Ann Futrell	Daniel Ready
Heidi Golding	Dawn Sauter Regan
Mark Grabowicz	Robert Stewart
Kathleen Gramp	Aurora Swanson
Raymond Hall	Natalie Tawil
Daniel Hoople	Martin von Gnechten
Dave Hull	Philip Webre
Justin Humphrey	Ellen Werble
Chung Kim	Susan Willie
Eric Labs	Dwayne Wright
Jeff LaFave	Rebecca Yip
Susanne Mehlman	

Revenue Options

Joshua Shakin of the Tax Analysis Division coordinated work on the options for revenues, which was done by the staff of the Joint Committee on Taxation and the following analysts:

David Austin	Robert McClelland
Mark Booth	Shannon Mok
Paul Burnham	Nathan Musick
William Carrington	Kevin Perese
Sheila Dacey	Charles Pineles-Mark
Nathaniel Frentz	Molly Saunders-Scott
Jennifer Gravelle	Kurt Seibert
Pamela Greene	Joshua Shakin
Ed Harris	Logan Timmerhoff
Janet Holtzblatt	

Health Options

Noelia Duchovny of the Health, Retirement, and Long-Term Analysis Division coordinated work on the options relating to health, which was done by the following analysts:

James Baumgardner	Carla Tighe Murray
Tom Bradley	Andrea Noda
Anna Cook	Lara Robillard
Stuart Hagen	Matthew Schmit
Daniel Hoople	Logan Timmerhoff
Sara Masi	Ellen Werble
Jamease Miles	Rebecca Yip
Eamon Molloy	

Appendix A

Ann Futrell of the Budget Analysis Division compiled Appendix A, with assistance from the following analysts:

Tom Bradley	Jeff LaFave
Megan Carroll	James Langley
Kim Cawley	Susanne Mehlman
Chad Chirico	Sam Papenfuss
Kent Christensen	Matthew Pickford
Sheila Dacey	David Rafferty
Sunita D'Monte	Joshua Shakin
Kathleen FitzGerald	Emily Stern
Kathleen Gramp	Aurora Swanson
Raymond Hall	Martin von Gnechten
Daniel Hoople	Jason Wheelock
Justin Humphrey	Susan Willie
Sarah Jennings	Dwayne Wright

Publishing

The production and publishing of the report were handled by CBO's web team, supervised by Deborah Kilroe, and the agency's editing and publishing group, supervised by John Skeen. Jeanine Rees edited the report, and Kate Kelly proofread it. Robert Dean, Annette Kalicki, and Simone Thomas prepared the electronic version of the report. Maureen Costantino designed the cover, and she and Jeanine Rees, with assistance from Allan Keaton and Rick Quatro, produced the printed version.